the perfect

party

the perfect *party* planner

**Hints, tips, advice and recipes to guarantee
success at every event – from birthday parties
and buffets to weddings and special celebrations**

bridget jones

southwater

This edition is published by Southwater,
an imprint of Anness Publishing Ltd,
Hermes House, 88–89 Blackfriars Road, London SE1 8HA;
tel. 020 7401 2077; fax 020 7633 9499

www.southwaterbooks.com; www.annesspublishing.com

If you like the images in this book and would like to investigate using
them for publishing, promotions or advertising, please visit our website
www.practicalpictures.com for more information.

UK agent: The Manning Partnership Ltd; tel. 01225 478444;
fax 01225 478440; sales@manning-partnership.co.uk

UK distributor: Grantham Book Services Ltd; tel. 01476 541080;
fax 01476 541061; orders@gbs.tbs-ltd.co.uk

North American agent/distributor: National Book Network;
tel. 301 459 3366; fax 301 429 5746; www.nbnbooks.com

Australian agent/distributor: Pan Macmillan Australia; tel. 1300 135 113;
fax 1300 135 103; customer.service@macmillan.com.au

New Zealand agent/distributor: David Bateman Ltd;
tel. (09) 415 7664; fax (09) 415 8892

ETHICAL TRADING POLICY
Because of our ongoing ecological investment programme, you, as our
customer, can have the pleasure and reassurance of knowing that a tree is
being cultivated on your behalf to naturally replace the materials used to
make the book you are holding. For further information about this
scheme, go to www.annesspublishing.com/trees

A CIP catalogue record for this book is available from the British Library.

Publisher: Joanna Lorenz
Senior Editors: Doreen Palamartschuk and Sarah Uttridge
Copy Editors: Jan Cutler, Jane Bamforth
Project Editor: Elizabeth Woodland
Production Controller: Claire Rae
Designer: Nigel Partridge
Jacket Design: Balley Design Associates
Photographers: Karl Adamson, Caroline Arber, Steve Baxter, Martin
Brigdale, Nicki Dowey, Gus Filgate, Michelle Garrett, Amanda Heywood,
Janine Hosegood, William Lingwood, Roisin Neild, Thomas Odulate, Spike
Powell, Craig Robertson, Simon Smith, Sam Stowell and Polly Wreford

Previously published as part of a larger volume, *Party Food*

Notes
Bracketed terms are intended for American readers. For all recipes,
quantities are given in both metric and imperial measures and, where
appropriate, measures are also given in standard cups and spoons.
Follow one set, but not a mixture, because they are not interchangeable.
Standard spoon and cup measures are level.
1 tsp = 5ml, 1 tbsp = 15ml, 1 cup = 250ml/8fl oz
Australian standard tablespoons are 20ml. Australian readers should
use 3 tsp in place of 1 tbsp for measuring small quantities of gelatine,
flour, salt, etc. Medium (US large) eggs are used unless otherwise stated.

Contents

Introduction

Party-giving should above all be enjoyable, and timely planning ensures that any event is as relaxed for the organizer as for the guests. This book aims to provide all the advice, guidelines and reminders you need to ensure that the planning is easy, the organizing smooth and problem-free, and the occasion a complete success – whether it's casual drinks party or a grand, formal wedding celebration.

Getting started

The process of deciding on dates, times, venues and occasion style often starts the roller-coaster task of putting

Below *To create a sophisticated look, choose one colour for napkins and table linen, and mix different textures such as linen and organdie.*

Above *Pure linen napkins add style and elegance to any dining table.*

together once-in-a-lifetime gatherings. It can often be a stressful time when you are making decisions such as whether traditional ceremonies take precedence over a relaxed celebration or how to assemble different groups of family and friends. Side-stepping a

frantic start helps to avoid dips in enthusiasm later on. Often the initial problems are not as complicated as they appear. Enthusiasm and energy are the first requirements for overcoming any uncertainties, backed up by making useful lists such as key dates, numbers of guests, types of food and drink. It is important to do this before any celebration, large or small, in advance of getting down to the practicalities of invitation writing, room clearing, cooking and greeting.

Enlisting support

There is no point in playing the party hero and trying to juggle every last item alongside a normal busy life – it is far more sensible and fun to share the load and satisfaction with at least one helper, if not a team of supporters.

Hand pick a reliable and hard-working friend who shares your aims, ethos and humour to join in the process – most people are flattered to be asked for their support, especially on important occasions. Then be thoughtful about who to add to the team. For children's parties, unless the occasion is a surprise, involve the child whose party it is and allow one special friend to be included in the pre-party organization.

Getting together a round-table of enthusiastic organizers is best avoided unless there are specific, separate tasks that are ideal for distributing among several contributors. Finally, there are times when coordinating a committee of people is an essential part of putting together a group event, such as for a club or school, and adopting the same approach to selecting one or two main helpers while ensuring everyone else is usefully involved is an excellent ploy.

Mix and match

If the occasion is very formal, such as a wedding or christening, or the approach so traditional that there is little room for changing the style and form, it is best to follow the rules of etiquette. For all parties adopt a sensible attitude to all numbers, catering, ambience and entertainment and use tried and tested approaches to ensure success.

Below *Add atmosphere to a party with floating candles in a glass bowl.*

When the occasion allows for flexibility, do not take yourself too seriously but aim for enjoyment rather than perfection. Mixing and matching can be an inspiring approach to party planning, especially for informal events. Adopt the "do it with a good will or not at all" approach and loosen up on the rules. Concentrate on the aspects you most enjoy. Those who are not keen on cooking for crowds often do best by selecting just one or two practical one-pot dishes and complementing them with well-chosen bought foods. There is plenty of advice on making the most of bought ingredients in the following chapters.

The same goes for party drinks: while all the experts may dictate offering chilled champagne or certain wines and liqueurs to go with individual courses during a meal, or an eclectic array of drinks, if you – or your budget – dictate otherwise, then do so with conviction and without apology. And if you want guests to make a contribution by bringing a

Above *Classic cocktail glasses will impress your guests at drinks parties.*

bottle, do not be afraid to make the occasion a "bring a bottle party" by spelling it out on the party invitations.

Enjoy!

Great atmosphere is the most important feature of any party or celebration – and that does not mean ambience alone. Whether you are entertaining in a palace or on a building site, remember to do so with a genuine and warm welcome. Make your guests aware of the type, context and style of the party so that they all come suitably dressed and in the right frame of mind to enjoy themselves. Greet everyone and be sure to encourage them to mingle, making them feel relaxed, at home and with a certain responsibility to participate. At the end of the day, no matter how brilliant the tables, food and decorations, it is the people who make the party.

party
planning

Approach successful entertaining with a clear sense of occasion and a
few concise, practical lists. Once you know what you are doing,
involve others in the fun and share the planning with friends or family.

Grand Design or Simple Style?

A clear picture of the party style and size is the secret of success every time. Before planning venues, invitations, settings, entertainment and food and drink, decide on exactly the right type of party. Energy and enthusiasm are essential for getting things moving but it is best to sort out guidelines within which to plan before ideas snowball and practicalities are forgotten in an initial wave of excitement.

There are established routines and etiquette for many occasions and utilizing these is often sensible. They range from formal dinner parties, society drinks gatherings or balls to weddings, anniversaries and seasonal gatherings. There are also just as many small or substantially large gatherings that are organized for no particular reason other than meeting up and socializing, for example overcoming winter blues, making the most of the summer sun or catching up with a group of friends.

Below An attractive buffet table with plates and napkins piled high.

Who's who?

Start with an outline guest plan: is this a gathering for six or sixty, under fives or over fifties, family or friends, bosom pals or business associates? If you are inviting a complete mix of family, friends, colleagues and neighbours a proper plan would be a sensible starting point. Identify the different types and ages; by fitting individuals into groups you will be sure to include something for everyone. This eases the role of host or hostess, which can involve looking after small groups or couples – or worse – individuals drifting about on the fringes of the party.

Time of day

The party may be to celebrate a marriage, baby naming or christening, or it may be a social event. It may not be a particularly jolly occasion, for example a post-funeral wake. Double-check arrangements that cannot be changed later, for example timings for ceremonies, photography or performances and estimated travelling time between event and party venue.

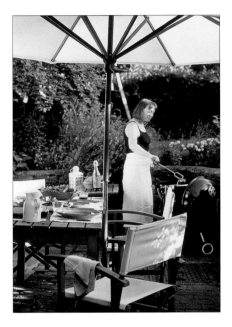

Above *Summer barbecues can be day or early evening social events.*

Consider the different ages of, or relationship between, guests before fixing times. A two-phase celebration is popular for very different groups; it would typically comprise a formal meal, low-key lunch or early evening drinks party followed by a lively gathering later for younger guests or close friends. This solution works as well for informal occasions – a house warming, open house for a summer barbecue or an annual family gathering – as for weddings. Plan the transition between day and evening, and decide whether those invited to the first part will also stay late.

Formal gatherings for early evening drinks preceding a late supper for a few friends or pre-lunch gatherings must be well orchestrated. Invitations should indicate the time when guests are expected to leave: "Pre-dinner drinks between 6 p.m. and 7.30 p.m." A verbal or informal note to join family or weekend guests for "a drink before lunch" should include the expected time of arrival and departure. Be clear to avoid any confusion.

Smarten up or dress down?

Once you know who and when, make a decision on how you want your guests to dress and behave, and follow this through in invitations, food and entertainment. Be clear on invitations if you expect formal dress (white tie and ball gowns; black tie and evening wear; morning wear, or top hats and tails, and hats), lounge suits or smart daywear. For an informal occasion dress will not need to be stipulated. Indicate any special requirements, such as bathing costumes and towels for poolside parties, sun hats and picnic blankets to sit on, and sweaters or shawls for evenings outdoors.

Before and after

Guests may need accommodation for the night before and/or after the party. After a long journey, house guests will usually want to arrive early enough to freshen up. Include the preparation of guests' rooms in your plans and timings, remembering the little things that make people feel welcome and relaxed – flowers, magazines, drinks, biscuits (cookies) or chocolates as well as towels, soap, shampoo and tissues. Keeping a few disposable, travel-size miniatures, or spare small toothbrushes, toothpaste, small packs of anti-perspirant and sachets of moisturizer in stock is a good idea for party guests who stay unexpectedly.

Pay attention to detail when entertaining youngsters, especially if they may be too shy to ask for forgotten essentials. For a special occasion sleepover you could prepare fun sleepover packs including novelty toothbrushes, fruit-flavoured toothpaste, wacky toiletries, expanding face cloths, reading material such as comics, mini torches, tasty midnight snacks and fruit, and small packs of drinks or bottles of water.

Above *Add romantic touches to a table dressed in white for a wedding.*

For large gatherings, check out local hotels and provide guests with details on price, location and availability when sending out invitations. Remember breakfast on the morning after the party and make flexible arrangements.

Party price

As each name is added to the guest list and every idea mulled and jotted bear in mind the cost. Decide on the type of party to suit the funds available, then work out a realistic budget in more detail before progressing from idea to plan. This is just as important for small, homely events as for once-in-a-lifetime occasions if you want to avoid overspending.

Sorting an outline budget at this stage is essential and easy: make a list of every aspect of the party, adding a realistic (generous rather than mean) cost and contacting suppliers to check special prices. For extravagant occasions involving hotels, venues, caterers, entertainers and so on, make specific enquiries at this first stage. Divide the costs into fixed amounts for the

occasion and variable prices that increase with the number of guests – refreshments in particular – remember that the venue size may change if the guest list grows too much. Spreading the cost by paying for some items, such as wine, spirits or beer, completely or partly in advance is one way of easing an overstretched budget, especially when planning a party at home.

Below *Simple snacks, drinks and bright decorations are good basics for a party.*

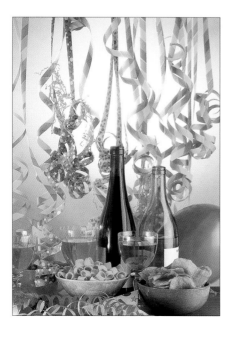

Have List, Will Organize

dinner parties and drinks parties are good Friday affairs, as are after-theatre or post-exhibition suppers.

Weekends are popular for group events for families and for activity club get-togethers or excursions. While weekend brunches are generally great for those without young children, Saturday brunch can also start family activities on a high note and the afternoon is a good choice for children's parties. If Saturday lunch is difficult for working hosts and guests who have to juggle family commitments, the evening is good

Lists are essential when planning for a special occasion. Suggesting that there should be a system for making them may sound like overkill but even the most super-efficient lists can become so mottled with additions that they become uninterpretable. The answer is to have separate lists with different information. Using a computer or a spiral-bound notepad is brilliant for keeping lists on separate pages but together in one place. Jot the date on each page and include notes of discussions with suppliers, orders placed and ideas as well as the guest list, special requirements, shopping and so on. Using this system it is easy to flip through to check details, and it is a good idea to sticker significant pages you refer to frequently, such as the invitation list where you will tick or

Above *Make lists for organizing all aspects of party planning.*

cross off guests' names as replies come in. Start with a list of the usual requirements for different occasions and then personalize it to your style.

Which day?
Work functions are best from midweek onwards. Friday can be a good day for lunch or an evening party if partners are invited; Wednesday or Thursday are more convenient for "colleague only" events (especially for a comparatively early finish).

Weekday dinner parties can be inconvenient but midweek evenings can be a good choice for drinks gatherings or supper parties designed to end early. Relaxed and informal

Above *Champagne is generally served at weddings and formal occasions.*

Below *One-pot feasts, such as moussaka, are good for supper parties.*

for large and/or formal dinner parties. Saturday is popular for weddings, allowing time for guests to travel; Friday is ideal when the marriage is witnessed by a small number of relations and followed by a party for friends and associates.

Sunday lunch is extremely versatile: it allows plenty of time for preparation and is suitable for informal or smart arrangements for family, couples, singles or a mixture.

Parties and celebrations for clubs and classes are usually planned for the day and time when the meetings are normally held. Annual dinners tend to be organized for Friday or Saturday evenings, depending on the work commitments of members.

Scheduling an important celebration

Lists should include all the details, whereas a schedule will set dates and deadlines for the tasks. Draw up a master schedule of key dates, tasks and reminders with references back to the lists for details where necessary. Lists can then be updated as time passes.

A few months may be enough time for organizing simple weddings but one to two years is usually allowed

Above *A stylishly dressed table for a Thanksgiving celebration.*

for extravagant affairs. Timing often depends on the booking requirements of venues and officials; check these carefully. Find out about caterers, entertainment and transport, and check the availability of all related aspects before booking the main event.

Put dates to the lists and check that they are all possible. Then draw up the outline schedule – the master guide to sourcing, booking, confirming and checking every aspect of the celebration. Schedule key dates for everything. Adding minor aspects may seem picky, particularly when coping with a big party, but they can easily be forgotten later. Use a familiar means of layout, if possible, be that a year planner, kitchen calendar, chart on a noticeboard or computer program.

Scrutinize your schedule for bottlenecks and potential problems. If too many tasks coincide make alternative arrangements by moving jobs to different dates or delegate them to helpers. When you are happy that you have not missed anything, make sure the schedule looks neat, tidy and is easy to follow.

Schedule checks

Below are items to add to the schedule according to the needs of the occasion, placing each against a date when it has to be done.

Formalities: legal/paperwork requirements, booking all officials, confirmation
Venue: viewing, booking, and confirmation, checking facilities, preparation
Entertainment: booking, venue preparation/layout requirements, details of repertoire
Accommodation: source details
Caterers: references/assessing, booking, menu decisions and/or tasting session, confirmation of numbers, caterer's advance visit
Special catering: special diets, finalizing details of presentation
Food preparation: ordering, shopping, key dates for advance cooking, days for final preparation
Bar: delivery/collection of drinks and glasses, return of items
Professional help at home: gardening, cleaning, kitchen help (before or after), butler, waiting staff, bar staff
Flowers: booking, venue visit and design liaison
Guest list: invitations out, give a date for replies back
Gifts: buy, pack

Choosing a Venue

The occasion, type and size of party, budget, convenience and availability all influence the choice of venue.

Home options

Entertaining at home can be stylish if there is suitable space. While clearing furniture to the edges of one or two small rooms and allowing everyone to spill into the hall and kitchen may be fine for an informal party, it is not necessarily the answer for a special celebration. Unless there is ample floor and table space plus kitchen facilities sufficient to cater for a sit-down meal, a buffet is most practical. When serving a fork buffet, remember that some guests may prefer to sit down to eat. When finger buffets or snacks are served, guests do not need as much space, especially if the refreshments are handed around.

Make use of outdoor areas and consider hiring an awning or marquee. Tables, chairs and barbecues can be arranged on firm areas; rugs and cushions can be laid on lawns. Be prepared for poor weather and consider erecting large umbrellas.

Below *With attention to detail, dressing a table at home can be very stylish.*

Hotels and restaurants

Select a venue by recommendation, reputation and personal experience if possible. Visit the restaurant for a meal to assess general quality and ambience. When comparing establishments, prepare a standard checklist and do not be embarrassed to make notes while you are there. The following are points to consider:

• How many guests can be catered for and in which room/bar. Check the maximum number of covers usually catered for; point out, if necessary, that you do not want their capabilities to be overstretched. Will a bar adjoining a function room be exclusively for the use of your party or will it also be open to the public? Check bar closing times.

Above *Put extra tables on patios and courtyards for home entertaining.*

• What types of menus are offered and at what price per head? What is included in the price per head? Are children's portions provided at reduced cost (prudent when a wedding guest list includes many children)?
• Do the regular kitchen staff prepare special functions, or are outside caterers or temporary chefs employed?
• Check wine lists and bar prices. Ask whether you will be able to supply your own wine or champagne and what corkage charge is applied?
• Check arrangements for overseeing the smooth running of the occasion and whether a master of ceremonies

is available. Ask about the suitability of spaces for speeches or if amplification equipment is available.

• Accommodation-wise, assess the number and type of rooms, and price per room/person, with or without breakfast. Ask if favourable rates will be offered for a block booking.

• Does the business have existing links with entertainers? At what time in the evening must music end? Are there particular florists who know the hotel/restaurant? Similarly, there may be a useful link with photographers who are familiar with the setting.

• Is the venue easily accessible by car or rail? Is there ample parking?

Hired hall or rooms

Community, sports, arts, social and religious venues often have rooms for hire. Some may have links with caterers, entertainers and dressers to prepare the venue (and you may be obliged to use bar facilities or caterers);

Below *Always visit hotel or restaurant venues to check the space and facilities before you book.*

accommodation may even be provided in some clubs. Less expensive venues are economical for self-catering. Points to check include:

• Heating (is this included in the cost?).

• Lighting and how it can be adapted to improve the ambience.

• Kitchen facilities for food preparation and storage, heating and clearing up.

• Tables and chairs – check how many there are, the table sizes and ensure they provide enough space for the number of guests.

• Bar facilities and whether alcohol is allowed; entertainment permits.

• Cloakroom facilities.

• Cleaning and preparation of venue – will the space be clear and clean? How far in advance will you have access for setting out tables, decorating the space, laying out food? Clearing up afterwards – will this have to be completed on the evening or next day?

Marquee hire

This may be a practical solution to gaining all-weather space if you have a large, flat garden. Hire companies provide guidance on size, numbers

Above *Brighten up hired tables with table linen and ribbons.*

accommodated and access required for erection. Erected sample marquees or a portfolio of examples should be available. Check the lining is intact, the flooring is solid, and there is provision for power, heating and lighting.

Picnics

These may be informal and fun, or formal social occasions attached to sporting or entertainment events. Follow custom and etiquette for society occasions, such as the serving of stylish hampers, or candlelit picnics in a country-house garden. When obtaining tickets for events, check details of times and facilities, parking (and distance from car park to picnic area), dress and conduct code.

Parties afloat

Boats range from floating restaurants and bars to those with facilities for extensive parties. Smaller vessels can be hired for small groups with or without professional staff, and entertaining up to a dozen friends with a champagne lunch or early supper is fun. Check that the company rigidly applies safety regulations – if in doubt seek advice from relevant local authorities. Inspect the vessel's facilities thoroughly. Check the duration and route of the trip and access and parking at or transport to the point of departure.

By Invitation Only

Common sense and consideration are vital for informal invitations while rules of etiquette apply to formal invitations. A note can sometimes follow informal verbal invitations or a telephone call of confirmation a couple of days in advance – typically when organizing dinner parties with friends. The timing for informal invitations depends entirely on how busy and flexible everyone is.

Invitation information

It may seem like a statement of the obvious but it is surprisingly easy to miss details or to include incorrect (conflicting) dates and days. Invitations need to include the following:

- Guest names, with correct titles.
- Host and/or hostess names.
- Occasion or reason for party.
- Venue.
- Day and date.
- Time: this may be approximate or precise. Before a formal meal, it is usual to indicate a period of about 30 minutes

Below *Simple themes work best when making your own invitations.*

The right time

- Breakfast may be arranged from early until mid morning.
- Coffee mornings are usually scheduled for 11 a.m.
- Brunch can be planned for any time from mid morning to early lunch, between usual breakfast and lunch times.
- Lunch is usually arranged at 12.30 p.m. or 1 p.m. but invitations may be for an early or late lunch.
- Afternoon tea invitations are often scheduled for 3 p.m. or slightly later. Children's tea usually follows the end of afternoon school, usually about 4 p.m.
- Supper is often early or late evening, indicating a light menu rather than dinner.

during which guests are expected (within the first 15 minutes). The time may include the expected duration of the gathering or a time when an evening will end – expressed as "carriages at …" on formal dinner invitations.

- Cocktails and drinks are served from 6 p.m. to 8 p.m.
- Dinner is usually served from 7.30 p.m. until 8.30 p.m., with invitations requesting the arrival of guests about 30 minutes beforehand for pre-dinner drinks.
- "At home" indicates a period of time during which guests may arrive and depart. This is informal and usually includes light nibbles and refreshments rather than a substantial or formal meal.
- "Open house" is the contemporary and particularly informal version of "At home", often extending from lunch (or mid-morning brunch) through to the evening and intended for a mix of families, friends and colleagues of all ages.

- RSVP (*répondez s'il vous plaît*), sometimes with a date, is a polite way of reminding guests that a reply is required.
- Address, telephone and other contact details for replying.
- Dress code and any other information: white tie indicating wing collars, white ties and tails for men, ball gowns for women; black tie and dinner jacket is standard evening wear for men, when women may wear long or short dresses. Notes on a party theme or other special dress requirements should be included.

Formal invitations

Written requests for the company of guests at a notable occasion are sent at least a month in advance. This is typical of family celebrations, such as weddings, when four to six weeks' notice is practical. (Key guests should be aware of the date well in advance.) Parties organized around public events may be arranged three to six months

Above *Stationery for formal occasions comes in many different styles.*

in advance. Check the closing date for confirming numbers when booking a venue, confirm with suppliers and ensure invitations are sent out in good time in order for replies to be returned by the required date.

The right title

Addressing guests by an incorrect title may cause offence. Check with the households or offices of those in public or official roles. There are reference books detailing all contemporary and traditionally correct forms of address and greeting, including academic qualifications, religious orders and positions, military ranks, titled persons and those of any office requiring recognition. When in doubt about how acquaintances and relatives prefer to be addressed, check with them, if possible. Otherwise, close family or friends may be able to advise.

Traditionally, a married woman takes the name or initials of her husband when addressed singly or as a couple, for example Mr and Mrs John Smith, Mrs John Smith or Mrs J. Smith. However, some object to this,

preferring to use their first name, and women may retain their own family name after marriage, choosing the title Ms instead of Miss or Mrs. Addressing unmarried couples as "Mr and Mrs" is usually unacceptable to them and both names should be used.

Inventive invitations

Dress the message up according to the type of party. Concentrate on style and quality for all invitations, from heavy flat cards with fine lettering and discreet decorative edging to bright folded cards that may be fun but fall short of becoming garish.

When using professional designers and printers ask to see samples and prices per quantity and remember that selecting from their usual repertoire may be more convenient and more successful than asking them to create something different and complicated. Craft techniques, art skills or calligraphy can be used to make invitations and party stationery. Involve the children when preparing fun invitations for junior events.

A personal computer can be used to design and print stationery to professional standards. If the printer is not likely to deliver the required quality

Above *Good quality paper and simple decorations make pretty invitations.*

in terms of colour and graphics, ready-printed paper, cards and matching envelopes can be used as a base for black-and-white printing.

Finally, creative flair and technology are by no means essential, as ready-printed party stationery is available from quality stationers and general stores. Neat handwriting is all that is required to add individual details.

Below *For formal occasions, take care to use the correct titles for guests.*

Equipment and Materials Lists

Make lists of all equipment needed at the outset to ensure that everything is readily available, budgeted and scheduled. This applies when entertaining at home, particularly for self-catering. When caterers are commissioned they will usually source all equipment related to preparing and serving the food, often including tables and chairs. If you have particular ideas let them be known in advance.

Buying or hiring?

Hiring is often the only practical option for large celebrations. However, if you regularly entertain medium-size gatherings at home it may be worth buying a basic kit. For example, good quality white china, plain glassware and dishwasher-safe standard cutlery are often available from factory outlets. Plain white flat sheets are an alternative to table linen and perfectly presentable when dressed up for the occasion. For informal, family and children's parties it is worth buying rigid plastic plates and

Above *Table linen, napkins and glassware can all be hired.*

dishes that can be stacked in the dishwasher rather than spending almost as much on disposable ware that will be used just once. Sort out stackable, covered storage boxes at the same time so that "the kit" can be packed away afterwards for use next time.

Large items

Tables and chairs are usually included in the hire fee for halls. Check numbers and condition when booking, making sure that they all stand securely when opened. For parties at home, it is usually possible to utilize or borrow spare household or garden tables but chairs can be more of a problem. Hiring folding or stacking plastic chairs may be the answer.

Remember protective floor coverings for pale or precious carpets, especially when planning an indoor–outdoor party with guests of all ages. Specialist non-slip coverings can be useful in hallways or over areas of carpet by the patio or French doors.

When planning a large barbecue party, consider hiring large gas or charcoal barbecues from caterers' suppliers. They will make cooking lots of food easier than coping on the minimum of space on the home barbecue. Outdoor gas heaters can also be hired.

Left *Plain white linen napkins can be decorated with fresh flowers.*

Below *Make sure the barbecue is large enough to cater for all your guests.*

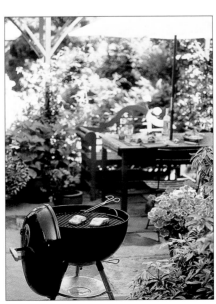

Check availability of entertainment equipment, such as inflatable play centres or bouncy castles, when fixing the party date, to avoid disappointment. Ask if the equipment will be assembled or inflated on delivery or left for you to erect, in which case make sure the necessary tools are also provided.

Food preparation and serving equipment

Catering hire specialists provide everything from disposable items to starched table linen and napkins, china and cutlery and serving equipment, including folding tables and chairs. When making your lists, sort requirements by category and then check outstanding queries with the hire store. Count and check equipment when taking delivery to make sure that it is all clean, present and undamaged. If there is anything dirty, missing or damaged, let the company know immediately otherwise you may be held responsible and charged for the problem at the end of the hire period. Most of the following items can be easily hired:

Below *Check in advance that you have all the cooking equipment you need.*

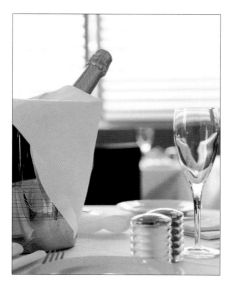

Above *Champagne flutes, ice buckets and cruets can all be hired for parties.*

• Cooking pans, trays and dishes – make sure your oven and burners are large enough to accommodate them.
• Coffee makers and water boilers.
• Serving bowls, trays and dishes – compare the cost of high-quality disposable items with hire charges.
• Table crockery – make a list from the menu, remembering cruets and sauceboats, if necessary, and cups, pots and spoons for coffee. Water jugs (pitchers) and glasses may be included with table crockery.
• Glassware may be hired or borrowed free of charge from wine suppliers or supermarkets – this may include spirit and beer glasses.
• Table linen, napkins and cutlery, plus serving cutlery.

All the trimmings

List all the decorative trimmings and finishing touches:
• Room decorations and streamers; garden decorations.
• Plants and/or decorations for patio and garden.
• Decorative indoor or outdoor lighting; candles or garden flares.
• Outdoor fireworks.

Above *Bright streamers and party hooters jazz up a birthday party table.*

• Table decorations, separated into fresh or silk flowers and others, such as coloured strings, confetti, candles, party poppers, whistles, bubbles, table crackers, indoor sparklers and other mini indoor fireworks.
• Balloons or balloon decorations.
• Guest gifts or children's goodie bags to take away and party-game prizes.
• Small cake boxes.

Below *Children love brightly coloured goodie bags to take home.*

Table Etiquette, Settings and Style

For formal occasions the host and hostess take their places at the ends of the table, with the most important male and female guests on their right (male to host, female to hostess). The remaining guests are seated in order of rank alternating male and female. When there is a master or top table, the most important guests take centre place. This arrangement is adopted for weddings, with the bride and groom in the middle, flanked by their parents and in-laws, with chief bridesmaid and best man at the ends.

Couples are usually seated opposite each other, the idea being that conversation flows around the table, not across it. When the numbers of men and women are equal, they are seated alternately around the table.

Above *Make sure there is ample elbow-room between each table setting.*

Below *Coloured modern cutlery mixed with elegant antique silver pieces.*

Seat people who are likely to have something in common next to each other. It is considerate to avoid pairing individuals whose opinions clash dramatically. When placing guests among several tables, try to achieve a compatible but interesting mix on each table. When there are children at formal occasions, it is sensible to put them on tables near the entrance, for easy cloakroom access. Guests with babies or small children may need space for prams or high chairs.

Make sure the writing on place cards is large enough to be legible by guests as they walk around the table. Display a seating plan on a board near the entrance to dining areas at large formal gatherings.

Formal table settings

The simple rule for formal settings is to lay cutlery for opening courses on the outside, starting from the right, and work in towards the plate.

• Use a large dinner plate to check the space for each setting and leave plenty of elbow-room between settings.

Above *Use traditional etiquette to avoid confusion: cutlery is placed on either side of the plates in order of courses.*

• Working from the right, lay the bread knife, soup spoon, fish knife or small side knife for the first course, large knife for the main course and dessert-spoon. Working in from the left, lay the fish fork or small fork for first course, fork for main course and dessert fork.

• For slightly less formal arrangements, the dessertspoon and fork may be laid across the top of the setting, spoon at the top (on the outside), with its handle to the right and fork below (on the inside), with its handle to the left.

• Cheese knives and utensils, such as a lobster pick or escargot tongs, may be brought in with the appropriate course. The cheese knife may be laid across the top, below the dessertspoon and fork.

• Arrange glasses at the top right above the setting in the order in which they are used. Include a water goblet or tumbler, white and red wine glasses.

• Distribute serving cutlery, cruets and butter dishes evenly around the table.

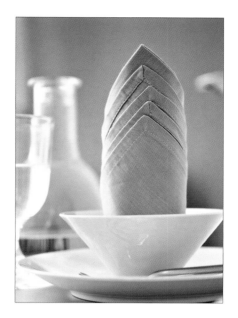

Above *Chevrons are just one way of folding linen napkins.*

Below *Cutlery can be bound together to add interest to an empty bowl.*

Contemporary style

Flaunt convention to make a design statement. The civilized rule when exploring new table-laying territory is to be practical and avoid confusing diners or causing embarrassment. If the cutlery is not laid in conventional positions it should be clear for which course it is intended. Bread knives can be laid on side plates, cutlery for the first course can be laid on a base platter with a napkin or brought in with the food, leaving the main course cutlery on the table. For stark effect leave the table bare, laying perfectly starched linen napkins at each place and bring out cutlery as courses are

served. Go for graphic lines and clean textures on table decorations, including any flowers and candles.

Base platters that remain in position under plates for first course and main course look attractive. They should be significantly larger than, and comfortably hold, the main-course plate so that it does not rattle. Glass, metal, wood or china in bold colours look especially dramatic under white or black plates. Match napkins to the base platter, arranging them on top as part of the setting.

Fun and lively

Strew the table with streamers and fun decorations in carefully coordinated colours. Bold flower petals and succulent leaves make a change from the usual floral decorations. Crystals, beads and glass baubles can be used to good effect in centrepieces or corner decorations. Use low or very tall candles to create pools of light. Make sure they do not block the view. Add crackers and indoor table fireworks for lively intervals between courses.

Below *Outdoor entertaining can be formal and stylish.*

Above *A wide selection of novelty items are available for children's parties.*

Mix and match

Ultimately, the best parties and meals are those where good food and entertaining company are shared in a relaxed atmosphere.

Mixing and matching food, table style and room setting can result in a wonderfully eclectic party. There is no reason why all the china, glassware, cutlery and linen should match; picking out one colour to use for decorations will transform a complete muddle of equipment into a lively style.

Presentation and Buffets

Reflect the style in atmosphere and presentation, from the first impression on entering the house to the lingering memories of an enjoyable party.

Formal sit-down meals
Give guests something to dress up for, balancing a sense of occasion and ceremony with a formal but relaxed atmosphere.

• The home or hired venue should be sparkling clean, sweet smelling and attractive with flowers or appropriate decorations. Aim for understated sophistication. Every area that guests will notice must be pristine.

• The table is the centrepiece, so devote time to planning it. Coordinate colour, shape and texture in decorations and presentation. Lay the table well in advance rather than as an afterthought. Lighting should be flattering, rather than bright, but never gloomy. Candlelight is perfect, so use candles around the room and set fairly low on the table or well above eye level of seated diners.

• The dining area should be pleasantly warm rather than uncomfortably hot. Be ready to reduce heating discreetly or provide ventilation as everyone warms

up over a meal, then to warm the room again later, if necessary.

• If possible, allow a beautiful table to be appreciated before everyone sits down. Leave the door to the prepared dining room open so that guests catch a tantalizing glimpse as they arrive. Allow time for seating guests at the table rather than rushing them.

Buffet basics
You can decorate the edge of a buffet table with flowers, garlands, bows or other trimmings. Table coverings and

Above *Highly decorative floral displays look good on buffets.*

edges can be flowing but they must not be so long that they become a hazard as people pass close by.

A fork buffet should include food that is easily eaten with just a fork. Plates should be arranged at one end of the table so that guests move along and help themselves. Displaying forks, napkins and any accompaniments on a small table slightly away from the end of the buffet will encourage guests to move away from the food. Buffet tables are often placed against a wall but moving the table into the room is better, encouraging guests to walk around and serve themselves without having to stretch over dishes.

If the buffet is self-service, all the food should be easy to serve with a spoon, tongs or slice using one hand. Try to arrange food in dishes of different heights, and display one or more large dishes as centrepieces.

Arrange food in a logical order rather than randomly on the table. Moving guests from main dishes on to

Left *A silver and white theme creates a classy dining table.*

accompaniments is logical if the menu takes that form. Replenish or replace dishes as necessary.

When the food takes the form of a main course, rather than a collection of complementary dishes, the savouries are usually cleared away before sweet dishes are brought out. This can be awkward in large gatherings if some guests are ready for dessert before others have finished the main course, so setting out cheese and desserts on a separate table is better.

Fabulously simple

Instead of setting out one large buffet table, you can distribute dishes individually among several occasional tables, adding a stack of small plates, forks and paper or linen napkins in each case. This is a brilliant way of presenting an eclectic collection of dishes, each to be sampled and savoured alone. Reflect the stylish approach by serving beautifully displayed food on plain white plates and keep decorative room trimmings uncluttered, just one step on from minimalism.

For this approach, the trick is to keep "waves" of prepared foods in reserve in the kitchen. Instead of laying them all out at once, replace empty platters as the food is consumed. Moving from one style of food to another is easy – rather like serving different courses of a meal – and it is a good idea to allow a palate-clearing pause between one variety and the next. For example, a range of marinated seafood may be followed

Above *Decorate a table for an autumnal lunch with fruits of the season.*

by a selection of roasted miniature vegetables and accompanying dips, and finally by the finest home-made chocolate truffles. Remember the rule: less is more.

Informal and fun

It is easy to lose a sense of style when casually decorating a home and displaying an informal buffet. Focus on a limited choice of fun decorations and controlled use of colour to avoid overdoing it with garish clutter.

Presenting just a small number of seriously delicious dishes or one or two types of the finest-quality ingredients is much more sophisticated than laying out an ill-matched mix of home-made and bought bits and pieces. For example, perfect seafood paella, a tureen of superlative soup and glorious platters of charcuterie and cheese will each make a fabulous meal when served with lots of fresh home-made bread and a herb-filled leafy salad.

Left *Bright table linen and plates complemented by colourful utensils add up to informal Mediterranean style.*

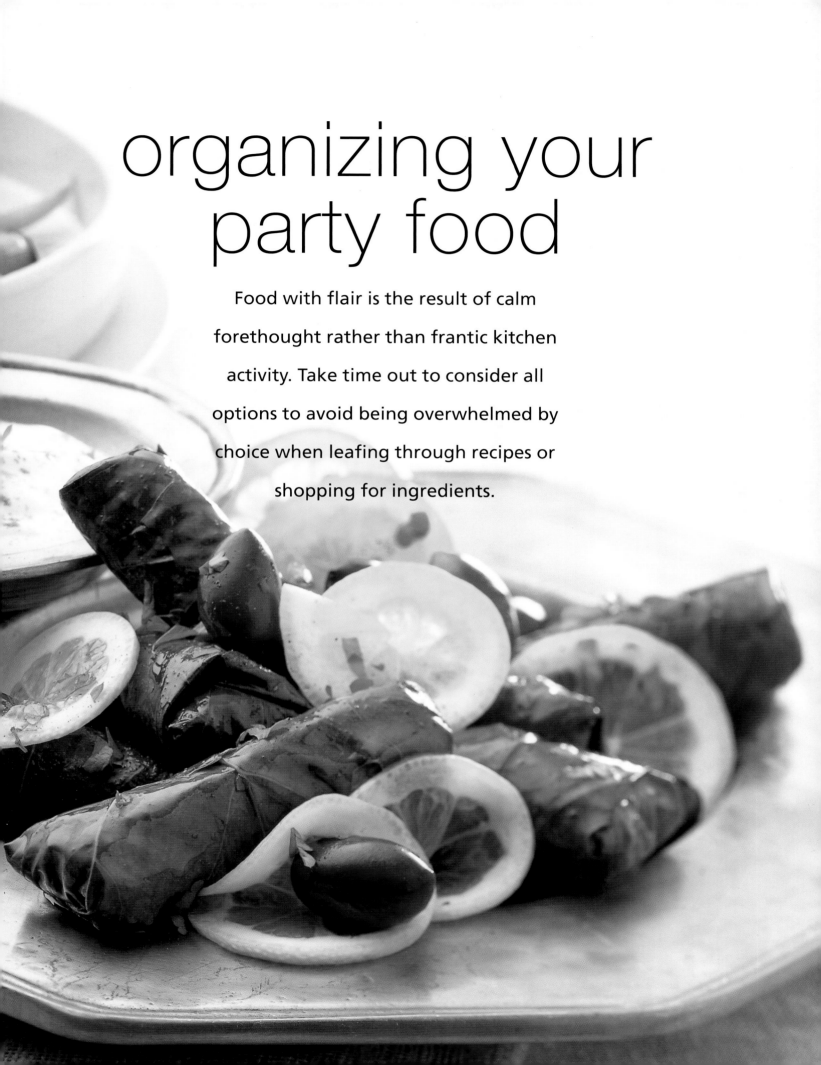

organizing your party food

Food with flair is the result of calm forethought rather than frantic kitchen activity. Take time out to consider all options to avoid being overwhelmed by choice when leafing through recipes or shopping for ingredients.

Planning Points

The easiest way to ensure a successful party is by tailoring your requirements to a suitable list of key points. Consider the following planning points:

• The occasion and type of meal are good starting points. Is the celebration formal or informal? Is it for adults or children, or both? Are you serving nibbles and finger food, a fork supper or a sit-down meal? A mixture of dishes can come together successfully as refreshment without fitting into accepted menu courses and this is true for seated eating as well as stand-up situations.

• Numbers and special requirements are important. Thinking up a menu that is over-ambitious to cook for a large number of guests can lead to disaster. An extravagant spread of many courses that is suitable for a dozen guests to sample in small quantities may be difficult to prepare and leave some guests embarrassed not to have done

Above *Lobster Thermidor and fillets of turbot with oysters are stylish dishes for special occasions.*

justice to the food. You should plan to accommodate special diets right from the beginning, for example, include vegetarian, vegan, or low-fat dishes on the menu. If guests have specific needs – such as gluten-free food – it is easier to plan suitable dishes as part of the main menu rather than preparing a set of alternatives at the last minute.

• Facilities should come high on the list of considerations. When finishing or serving food away from home, at a hired venue, or a picnic for example, make sure that every dish can be transported, reheated or cooked at the venue as appropriate. Check out facilities available at the venue, if necessary. At home, the danger is overstretching facilities, so avoid planning too many dishes requiring

last-minute cooking or heating to fit in the oven or for the top of the stove. Some recipes cooked at different temperatures cannot be adapted for cooking in the same oven. Also make sure you have enough crockery and cutlery for the menu.

• Food options are endless, so cost and capabilities are vital. When buying ready-made or commissioning caterers be aware of prices before dreaming up a menu to blow the budget. When planning to cook, work within your capabilities; being adventurous is fun within reasonable limitations but beyond this it can become a problem. Enlist the help of others or combine bought and home-made to be practical when there is a lot to be done.

Money can evaporate when using expensive ingredients and it is easy to isolate a pricey shopping list and get carried away, forgetting that it all adds up with drinks and other party costs.

Match courses or dishes

For formal menus, plan courses that complement each other and balance substantial and light dishes. The same criteria apply to finger or fork buffets, but there is more flexibility when guests don't have to eat dishes in order.

Below *Tarts and quiches are popular choices for a buffet or brunch.*

Selecting recipes

Confident cooks who entertain often and enjoy providing culinary theatre for guests may opt for lots of last-minute cooking, especially when they have kitchen space to accommodate spectators. Otherwise it is sensible to plan the menu around cook-ahead dishes, with last-minute cooking limited according to ability and the occasion. Being with your guests at a dinner party is important, while doing whirling dervish impressions between stove and buffet table can be stressful for both partygoers and you. Consider the following points:

• Balance hot and cold dishes to minimize last-minute work. One or two hot dishes are usually sufficient for a formal, main-meal buffet.

Above *Cut the first slice of cakes so guests can then easily help themselves.*

• Go for recipes based on familiar techniques.
• Select dishes that are practical to serve as well as prepare.
• For stand-up buffets, avoid dishes that are difficult to eat with only a fork.
• When arranging a finger buffet, select foods that are bitesize or easy to handle and bite without being messy.
• Leafy salads fill plates and can be difficult to eat when standing up, so guests tend to take less from buffets. Serve dressings separately from salads

that are likely to wilt so that they can be added to taste when served; this prevents the salad from become soggy.
• Creamy salads and dishes that can be piled neatly on plates or in which ingredients cling together are popular.

Increasing quantities

Recipes that can be increased in quantity successfully include soups, casseroles, sauces for pasta and recipes for individual portions (such as a specific number of chicken portions).
• When increasing the volume of stews and casseroles by more than three times, re-assess the volume of liquid as the proportion can be reduced slightly.
• Pies with pre-cooked fillings and a lid can be made in larger portions and cooked in larger dishes without vastly increasing the cooking time.
• Baked pasta dishes (such as lasagne or cannelloni) are excellent candidates for cooking in quantity.
• It is easier to boil large quantities of pasta in separate batches than to try to overfill a pan. Undercook it very slightly, drain and rinse, then toss with a little olive oil and reheat briefly in a suitable covered dish in the microwave.
• When increasing quantities by more than double, do not multiply up the herbs, spices and garlic several times as they may become overpowering.

Above *Baked dishes, such as lasagne, are good choices for supper parties.*

• Accompanying sauces for hot dishes and dressings for salads do not have to be increased by as much as the main ingredients when increasing the recipe by more than two or three times.

Menu cards

Displaying a menu card is an excellent way of letting everyone know what they will be eating or identifying dishes on a buffet. Arrange several menus on a large buffet table and remember to identify those dishes that are suitable for vegetarians or special diets.

Below *Use bought or home-made menu cards to identify buffet dishes.*

Cooking Plans, Shopping and Storage

With the menu organized it is time to get down to practicalities and, yet again, making the right lists eases everything along.

Cooking plan

Make a list of all the cooking. It is a good idea to copy the recipes and keep them together in a plastic folder in the kitchen when preparing them.

Divide the list into those recipes to cook well in advance and freeze, adding notes on when to remove them from the freezer, with likely thawing time and any finishing touches or reheating time. Note down any seasonings or enriching ingredients that have to be added at the last minute and include this on the checklist of things to do.

List the dishes that have to be cooked just before the party, that is the day before or on the same day. Note any advance preparation next to each dish. For example, salad dressings can be made a day or two ahead and chilled; some salad ingredients can be trimmed or peeled and washed the day before, then chilled ready for use – spring onions (scallions), celery sticks and tomatoes are good examples.

When all the dishes are listed, with the days on which they have to be made, it is then easier to draw up a cooking plan. Order the recipes according to the day on which they have to be made, then go through this list to make sure it is all possible. If you have far too much work for any one day, check whether any can be made in advance. If you have chosen too many last-minute dishes, adjust the menu before embarking on a shopping spree.

On your cooking plan, list different items to be prepared separately – this way you are less likely to underestimate the work involved. As well as volume of work, make sure that you have enough containers, work surfaces and note the cooking appliance needed for each dish.

Shopping lists

Working from numbers and menu, check the recipes and increase the quantities if necessary. Then work out

Above *Use good quality meat cuts and poultry from the butcher's.*

Below *Keep fresh fish and shellfish chilled until ready to cook.*

the shopping list, checking store-cupboard ingredients. Rather than having one mammoth list, divide it according to type of food, items that can be bought in advance and perishable last-minute purchases. Include any notes, reminders or alternatives on the lists to make shopping as efficient as possible.

Orders and deliveries

Scrutinize the list for items that should or can be ordered: meat cuts from a local butcher; fish to be prepared by the fishmonger; bread to be reserved at the supermarket or ordered from the baker and so on. Take advantage of delivery services offered by super-

Left *Local greengrocers may deliver fresh fruit and vegetables to your door.*

Above *Use temporary containers as colourful ice buckets.*

Below *Defrost frozen items slowly and then keep them cool.*

markets and organic produce that can be bought over the Internet. Do not be shy about asking for a delivery from local suppliers if you are placing an exceptionally large order.

Seek out mail-order suppliers for specialist or fine quality ingredients. Virtually all foods are available by this method and it is a particularly good option for specialist items, such as excellent raw or baked hams or high quality fish and shellfish.

Keeping cool and safe

Check refrigerator and freezer space well in advance. If you are cooking and freezing dishes ahead, make sure you have plenty of storage space. Sort and clean the refrigerator. Assess the amount of storage space you need and sort out practical options – a helpful neighbour

may have refrigerator space or, in cold weather, an unheated utility room or a suitable clean, dry outside area can be useful for less perishable items.

• Chill bottles of wine, beers and soft drinks in a large, clean plastic bin or several buckets part-filled with water and ice.

• Use chiller boxes and ice packs when the refrigerator is full – borrow or buy these in advance.

• Make temporary chiller boxes by lining rigid plastic stacking boxes with double-thick, heavy bubble wrap and covering the bottom with ice packs or ice in sealed plastic bags. Place on the floor in a clean, safe and cool area to hold ingredients or less-delicate dishes. Cover the top with more ice packs to keep the cold in.

• Prioritize your refrigerator space for highly perishable food such as fish, meat, poultry and dairy products. Fish should be kept in the coldest section of the refrigerator.

• Cool cooked dishes as quickly as possible. Cover them securely and chill them promptly.

• Leave items to be served cold in the refrigerator until the last minute.

• Thaw frozen items properly, keeping them cool.

Above *Some kinds of vegetables can be prepared and chopped in advance.*

Coping with leftovers

There are inevitably leftovers after a large party. Being prepared for coping with them makes clearing up far easier. Buy plenty of large plastic bags and clear film (plastic wrap). Some foods, such as cheese, should be wrapped and chilled promptly. Transfer leftovers to suitably small containers, cover and chill. Leftover cooked vegetables or green salads can be transformed into delicious soup with a minimum of fuss.

Below *Wrap leftovers promptly after a meal and transfer to a refrigerator.*

Cook Ahead, Stay Calm

Meat and poultry sauces and casseroles

Hearty meat and game casseroles freeze well, for 3–6 months. Poultry casseroles using portions do not have as good a texture as when they are freshly cooked, but diced poultry casseroles and sauces freeze well. Mushrooms and crisp vegetables are not as good after thawing as when freshly cooked. Add some finely diced vegetables for flavouring the casserole during the cooking, then add more sautéed vegetables when reheating for a good texture. Fine-textured or minced (ground) meat sauces – bolognese, chilli con carne – are successful when frozen and thawed.

Left *Stocks, sauces and casserole dishes can often be cooked ahead.*

It may be possible to cook the majority of a meal or buffet in advance, spreading the work load over a period of time. You will then have it all ready in the freezer, leaving accompaniments and side dishes for last-minute preparation. Select the right type of dishes for success. Try some of the following ideas remembering that the freezer life depends on the ingredients used in the dishes more than the type of dish.

Soups

Smooth soups freeze well for up to three months. Do not add cream, yogurt, fromage frais or egg yolks before freezing. Reheat gently, then add the dairy ingredients before serving.

Pâtés

Smooth, rich pâtés freeze well for up to one month. They are best served sliced or scooped, as they can look slightly tired when served from the dishes in which they were frozen. Home-made pâtés and spreads (fish, poultry or meat) are excellent for topping canapés.

Above *Most soups and some types of sauces can be cooked in advance.*

Above *Cook meat sauces in advance and freeze until needed.*

Above *Make stocks and freeze in ice cube trays until ready to use.*

Above *Make curry pastes and sauces ahead of schedule.*

Stuffings

Breadcrumb, meat or fruit stuffings can all be frozen up to one month ahead. Rice is not so good as the grains soften and become slightly granular.

Sauces, gravies and dips

Reduced cooking juices and flour-thickened sauces and gravies freeze well for up to 3 months. However, those based on eggs and oils are not suitable, as they curdle. Finely chopped or puréed vegetable salsas are excellent freezer candidates. Home-made dips also freeze well – try avocado dips (guacamole), chickpeas and tahini (hummus), or roasted vegetables puréed with cream cheese. Light, mayonnaise-based dips do not freeze well as they tend to curdle.

Vegetable dishes

Although the majority should be freshly cooked, there are some useful dishes to freeze ahead. Creamy mashed potatoes and vegetable purées freeze well for up to 6 months – great for decorative gratin edges, pie toppings or reheated in the microwave and stirred before serving. (You will be amazed at how quickly fabulous mash disappears from a buffet – with butter, chopped fresh herbs and a little grated lemon rind mash is a delicious accompaniment and easy to eat.) Grated potato pancakes are also excellent: lay them out on a baking tray ready for rapid reheating and crisping in a hot oven. Firm vegetable terrines also freeze well for up to 1 month.

Pastries

Filled pastries should be frozen raw, then cooked at the last minute. Puff or filo pastries that are time-consuming to prepare but quick to cook are ideal. Buy chilled rather than frozen pastry. Brush shaped filo pastry with a little butter or olive oil (or a mixture) before

Above *Pipe mashed potato into scallop shells for Coquille St. Jacques.*

Above *Make samosas or small pastries in advance and freeze.*

freezing to prevent it from cracking. Cook small pastries from frozen. Large pastry items – pies, tarts, and pastry-wrapped fish – should be frozen raw and thawed before cooking. They will keep well for 1–3 months, depending on the ingredients in the filling.

Cooked choux pastries, such as profiteroles, freeze well unfilled. Crisp the pastries very briefly in a hot oven when thawed, then cool and fill. If serving savoury buns hot, fill then reheat them; depending on the filling, they may be filled before freezing and, if small, reheated from frozen.

Batters and baked goods

Pancakes are versatile; interleave them with clear freezer film (plastic wrap), then pack in a freezer bag. They keep well for a few months and are excellent filled with savoury or sweet mixtures, and baked. Baked sponge cakes, meringues, muffins and breads freeze

Above *Fish cakes can be made in advance and frozen individually.*

Above *Brush small savouries with a little melted butter before freezing.*

well also. Protect delicate items by packing them in rigid containers. Fill gâteaux and desserts when they are part-thawed.

Ices

You can prepare iced desserts up to a week or two in advance, but any longer and they can become "icy" with ice crystals. Richer mixtures keep better than lighter recipes: cream-rich parfaits frozen in moulds are a good choice.

Safe thawing

Thaw cooked dishes overnight in the refrigerator or a cool place and reheat to their original temperature. This is important for meat and poultry sauces.
• Defrost frozen items to be served chilled (pâtés, sponge cakes, gâteaux) in the refrigerator for up to 24 hours. Transfer delicate items to serving platters while frozen, cover and thaw in the refrigerator.

Simple Presentation

Anticipation of good food is an enjoyable part of the dining process, so creating a visual feast is as important as making food taste terrific. Getting the look just right for a smart dinner party is less daunting than creating a buffet that does not look messy or ridiculously over-elaborate. Achieving food that is easy to serve as well as appealing and delicious is the ultimate aim, and it is not difficult.

Appetizing presentation

Here are a few simple rules for food presentation – they apply to individual or large portions, fork suppers, dinner parties or buffets:

• Drips and drizzles should be wiped off dishes, especially cooking dishes.

• One or more folded clean dishtowels can be wrapped around hot dishes.

Above *Line bread baskets with crisp linen napkins.*

Below *Present hot serving dishes wrapped in clean napkins.*

• The serving dish should suit the food: neither too small nor too large, it should be deep enough to hold liquids without slopping, and large enough for items to be cut, scooped or spooned out without overflowing.

• Select dishes to complement the colour, shape and pattern of the food. Plain foods can be served on patterned crockery but fussy, bitty ingredients look best on plain designs or simple white crockery.

Appropriate garnishes

Any garnish should complement the food in style, flavour, texture, colour and shape. These finishing touches should enhance not mask the dish and they must not clash with the main ingredients.

Herb, vegetable and salad garnishes should complement the flavours of the dish or cooking style. For example, salad garnishes go well with pan-fried main courses and fairly dry bakes or pastries, but they are ghastly floating in a delicious hot sauce or gravy, where

Above *Serve appropriate sauces and accompaniments with each dish.*

they do nothing other than become limp and wreck the temperature, flavour and texture of the food.

Crisp croûtons, puff pastry shapes (*fleuron*) and shreds or shapes of pancake or omelette are all excellent for introducing contrasting shapes and textures. Nuts, roasted seeds and crisp-fried noodles or pasta shapes contribute texture. Diced or coarsely shredded potatoes, carrots and beetroot (beet) can be deep-fried to make delicious garnishes.

Divine decorations

Some good-looking sweet dishes are best left to make their own perfect statements with perhaps little more than a dusting of icing (confectioners') sugar – fabulous fruit salads, creamy roulades, whirly meringues, sparkling jellies and feather-light baked soufflés, for example. Others will benefit from a little decoration.

Sweet decorations should complement the main dish in colour, texture, flavour, style and form. The decoration should not overpower or clash with the dessert in any way. Be aware that it is easy to overdo the decoration on desserts, so avoid a cheap-looking concoction.

Many desserts are inherently decorative – set or baked in moulds, using decorative ingredients, topped with swirled cream, or served with colourful fruit sauces. A minimalist hint at decoration is often all that is needed – a single strawberry leaf with a part-sliced fruit; a cluster of perfect red currants; the smallest mound of chocolate curls; a simple dusting of dark cocoa powder; or a tiny sprinkling of golden-toasted flaked (sliced) almonds.

Elaborate piped decorations may not make a contemporary fashion statement but they can be lusciously alluring when applied with style. The fatal mistake is adding one swirl too many. Instead of using a decorative nozzle, try a plain one or use a medium-size spoon to apply cream and a fork to swirl it lightly.

Buffet sense

When adding finishing touches to buffet food, keep individual dishes simple, remembering that they will make a mosaic of colour and form when they are together on the buffet. Make the food look approachable and easy to serve when you expect guests to help themselves, otherwise elaborate or awkward-looking creations will be avoided by all but the most confident.

• So that food is easy to reach, stagger the arrangement of dishes and do not overfill the table. Instead, top up plates or dishes or remove and replace empty dishes occasionally.

• Do not overfill dishes or platters.

• When possible, present individual portions of food that are easier to serve and make them smaller than you would for a sit-down meal as diners usually prefer to sample a range of foods from a buffet than to take a full-size portion of one dish.

• Cut large items into small portions and remove the first piece, resting it on a serving spatula or laying it on the first guest's plate. This applies to items such as quiches, pies, pizzas and gâteaux.

• When serving whole hams, roasted poultry or large pieces of meat, the best solution is to present the whole item, then make a display of carving the first batch as an invitation to guests to eat. Encourage everyone to cut as much as they require, check occasionally and enlist the help of a friend to check that enough is carved.

Food centrepieces

Buffet tables will benefit from some form of centrepiece, which is usually a large main dish or an elaborate dessert. Alternatively, a fabulous display of fruit

Above *Stunning cakes and tortes make good buffet centrepieces.*

or a superb cheese board arranged on a raised stand, with splendid breads and crackers in a huge basket all look good towards the back of a buffet table. These form a focal point and backdrop, and are ready to bring forward when the main course has been consumed; they also help to keep the buffet looking neat, whole and appealing.

Below *Raised dishes or platters save space on a buffet table.*

Garnishing and Decorating

The possibilities are endless, and much creative use can be made of the main ingredients in the dish, presenting them with a slightly different twist. These classic, simple ideas are versatile and effective.

Herbs

Sturdy sprigs sit well alongside main food, while fine, feathery sprigs can be placed on top. Tiny sprigs are best for small or delicate items.

• Chopped herbs bring fresh colour to soups, casseroles, sauces, rice, pasta and vegetables. As they also add flavour, they should be used with discretion. Neat lines of finely chopped herbs, applied from a large chef's knife, add dimension to large areas of pale and creamy mixtures.

• Fried parsley is delicious with fish and shellfish, and it brings crunchy texture to creamy sauced dishes. Wash and thoroughly dry small tender sprigs of curly parsley, then drop into hot deep oil and deep-fry for a few seconds until bright green and crisp. Drain well on kitchen paper.

Vegetables

Finely sliced vegetables, such as cucumber, (bell) peppers, carrots or tomatoes, can be overlapped in threes or arranged in groups.

• Julienne, or fine matchstick strips,

Below Bundles of herbs tied together can be used to garnish savoury dishes.

Above *Cut four lengths of chives and use another chive to tie them together.*

look good in neat little heaps or criss-cross rows. Root vegetables – carrots, beetroot (beet), potatoes or swede (rutabaga) – are good raw or cooked as appropriate. Other suitable vegetables include celery, courgettes (zucchini), fennel, peppers or cucumber.

• Fine dice of raw or cooked vegetables look good in rows or heaps. Adjacent rows of contrasting coloured vegetables look very smart.

• Ribbons pared using a potato peeler can be used raw or cooked, depending on the vegetables. Carrots and courgettes are ideal.

• Grated or shredded raw carrots, white radish or cooked beetroot look good heaped in tiny mounds or other neat arrangements.

• Decorative shapes can be cut from lightly cooked sliced root vegetables,

Below Chillies can be arranged as garnishes for hot and spicy dishes.

Above *Chopped fresh parsley sprinkled on savoury dishes is an effective garnish.*

sliced courgettes, blanched peppers, pared cucumber peel or the outer flesh and skin of quartered tomatoes. Use tiny aspic cutters or a small, very sharp knife.

Citrus shapes

Slices and wedges are easy and effective. Wedges are easier to squeeze if the juice is required to sharpen the food. Slices – whole, halved or cut into sections – are useful for sweet dishes.

• Twists are fine slices with a single cut from centre to edge and the cut edges separated in opposite directions.

• Shreds of citrus rind can be cut using a cannelle knife (zester). Simmer them in boiling water until tender, and then drain. For sweet dishes, quickly roll the shreds in caster (superfine) sugar and leave them on a board to dry.

Below Cut vegetables into fine strips to add a splash of colour.

Above *Cut small chillies with scissors or a sharp knife to make chilli flowers.*

Below *Make cucumber flowers by folding alternate cut slices inwards.*

Salad ingredients

A chiffonade of bright salad leaves makes an extremely fresh garnish. Roll one or two leaves together fairly tightly and use a sharp knife to cut the finest slices, then shake these out into shreds.
• Curls are highly decorative and slightly oriental. Shred spring onions (scallions), leaving the shreds attached at the root end. Pare short, thin, curly strips off carrots using a vegetable peeler. Cut fine julienne of celery. Place the prepared vegetables in a bowl of iced water and leave for at least 30 minutes, or until they curl.
• Tomatoes and red radishes can be decoratively cut to resemble flowers. Use a small, sharp, pointed knife and, starting at the base, make small "V"-shaped cuts with the points at the top. Make sure the flesh is still attached at

the wide base. Make another row of cuts around the base, and then continue making successive neat rows of cuts up to the top of the vegetable. Always curve the knife around the shape of the vegetable to keep the section of cut flesh evenly thin. Place in a bowl of iced water until the cuts open out to create a flower shape.

Vandyke is the name given to a zigzag cut used to divide radishes and tomatoes decoratively in half. Use a small, fine, pointed knife to make zigzag cuts around the middle, cutting in as far as the centre. Carefully pull the two halves apart. This technique is also useful for citrus fruit and apples; eating apples can be sprinkled with lemon juice and sugar and placed under a preheated grill (broiler) until the sugar turns golden and caramelizes.

Above *Individual twists of sliced lemon look good grouped together.*

Above *Tomato flowers are made by peeling back the skin of cut tomatoes.*

Breads

Croûtons, croûtes and croustades are all crisp and browned bread garnishes. Croûtons may be small, neat dice or hearty chunks; croûtes are thin or thick but fairly small slices served on the side or used as a base for serving main ingredients; croustades are small containers that can be filled with a variety of savoury mixtures.

Croûtons and croûtes are fried in a mixture of oil and butter. However, if the slices of bread are brushed with a little oil before being cut up they can be spread out on an ovenproof dish and baked until crisp and golden.
• To make croustades, cut thick slices of bread, then cut them into cubes or rounds and hollow these out neatly. Brush sparingly all over with a little oil and bake until crisp and golden.

Above *Brush croûtons with a little oil before baking.*

Above *Use a sharp knife to make ridges in avocados and then slice thinly.*

Pastries

Puff pastry shapes can be savoury or sweet: glaze savoury shapes with beaten egg before baking or brush sweet ones with a little egg white and sprinkle with sugar. Use aspic cutters or large pastry cutters to stamp out suitable shapes.

• Filo pastry shreds are decorative, crisp and delicious with savoury or sweet dishes that have a soft texture. Roll up the pastry, then cut it into 1cm/½in wide slices. Shake these out on to a greased baking sheet and brush with a little oil before baking until golden. Dust with caster (superfine) sugar for sweet decorations.

The shreds can be sliced more finely and arranged in neat nests to be filled with savoury or sweet ingredients.

Pancakes

Thin crêpes or pancakes make excellent garnishes for clear soups and leafy green salads. To cut shreds, tightly roll up one or two pancakes and with a sharp knife slice them into very fine or thin slices, then shake them out. Alternatively, use aspic or pastry cutters to stamp out shapes.

Below *Toasted coconut is a delicious decoration for many desserts.*

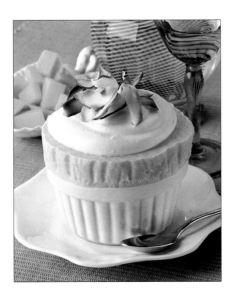

For sweet decorations, melt some unsalted (sweet) butter in a frying pan and cook the shreds or shapes, turning once or twice, for a few minutes, until crisp. Transfer to a board or plate and sprinkle with sugar.

Nuts, seeds and grains

Dry-fry nuts, seeds or grains in a heavy frying pan until they are lightly browned. Stir them constantly so that they brown evenly. Remove from the pan immediately. Use the nuts, seeds or grains to garnish soups, salads (savoury or sweet) or creamy desserts.

• Lightly toast nuts on a piece of foil under a medium-hot grill (broiler), turning them frequently so that they brown evenly. Use to garnish soups, salads, vegetables or sauced dishes. They are also good on desserts, gâteaux and ices. For sugary nuts, lightly toast halved blanched almonds, then immediately toss them with sugar and transfer to a plate to cool.

• Praline is made by tossing lightly roasted nuts, usually almonds, in caramel. Toast blanched almonds or hazelnuts under a grill or in a heavy, dry pan. Make a caramel sauce and stir in the nuts, then pour the mixture on to an oiled baking sheet. Leave to cool completely and set. Crush the praline with a rolling pin and use to decorate creamy desserts, gâteaux or ices.

Jelly garnishes and decorations

Aspic is the savoury jelly used to glaze chilled cold dishes or make attractive garnishes. Available in packet form, for either fish or poultry, or made by adding dissolved gelatine to clarified fish or chicken stock, set the jelly in a thin layer in an oblong container. Use aspic cutters to stamp out tiny shapes or turn the jelly out on to a board and chop it neatly. Aspic can also be set on sliced black or stuffed green olives,

Above *Fresh seasonal fruits look stunning on this Genoese sponge cake.*

herb sprigs or tiny colourful vegetable shapes in ice cube trays.

• Fruit jelly, home-made or from a packet, can be set and cut into shapes or chopped as for aspic. It can also be set over pieces of fruit in ice cube trays.

Creamy finishes

Whipped cream can be swirled or piped over desserts using a decorative or plain nozzle. Small swirls make decorative edging while large and luscious whirls are good toppings for individual desserts. For a looser feel, drop spoonfuls of cream on to the dessert and sprinkle with chopped toasted nuts.

Below *Boston Banoffee pie decorated with piped whipped cream.*

Above *Iced Christmas torte with sugared leaves.*

Use double (heavy) or whipping cream. When whipping cream, make sure it is well chilled and use cold utensils, then whip it until it stands up in soft peaks – slightly softer than you need as it firms when piped or spooned. Swirled cream provides contrast and interest in savoury or sweet dishes, such as smooth soups and fruit or chocolate sauces. Trickle a little single (light) cream into the dish, then drag it slightly with a cocktail stick (toothpick).

Feathered cream is attractive in sauces. Drop small dots of cream into the sauce, then drag them with a cocktail stick into feather shapes.

Sugared decorations

These are effective as decorations on all sorts of sweet dishes. Select tiny bunches of currants, small whole fruit or edible flowers, such as rose petals, and small leaves from mint, scented geraniums or blackcurrants. Make sure the fruit or flowers are clean and dry.

Lightly whisk a little egg white and brush over the fruit or flowers, then dust generously with caster (superfine) sugar. Transfer to a wire rack and leave until crisp and dry.

Chocolate shapes

Melted plain (semisweet), milk or white chocolate can be used to make a variety of shapes. Melt the chocolate in a bowl over a pan of hot, not boiling, water. Pour the chocolate on to a board covered with baking parchment, then spread it out evenly and thinly using a metal spatula. Leave until just set but not brittle.

Use cutters to stamp out shapes, and use a ruler and sharp knife to cut geometric shapes. Use a large, sharp cook's knife to make chocolate caraque or long curls: hold the knife at an acute angle and scrape off the surface of the chocolate in large curls. Transfer each curl to a separate board and leave until they are firm. To make chocolate leaves, instead of pouring the chocolate on to a board, brush it over the back of washed and dried perfect rose leaves. Apply two or three coats, then set the leaves aside to dry. Ease the leaves away from the chocolate once it has set.

Ice bowls

An ice bowl makes an impressive serving dish for ice creams and sorbets (sherbets). Make the bowl well in advance and store it in the freezer. Fill it with scoops of ice cream a few hours before dinner, return to the freezer and dessert is ready to serve at once!

Below *Serve ice cream or sorbets in a spectacular ice bowl.*

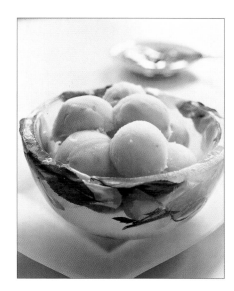

Making an ice bowl

1 Select two bowls, one about 5cm/2in smaller than the other. Stand a few ice cubes in the bottom of the larger bowl and place the smaller bowl on top so that the rims of both bowls are level. Tape the bowls at intervals at the edge. Slide slices of fruit or flowers between the bowls and pour in cold water to fill the gap.

2 Freeze the bowls. Use a skewer to push the fruit or flowers down between the bowls if they float during freezing. To release the ice bowl, remove the tape and pour a little hot water into the small bowl and stand the bottom bowl in hot water. As soon as the ice bowl is released place it in the freezer.

party themes

Make the most of every party opportunity by focusing on a particular approach. Whether the occasion demands etiquette and sophistication or relaxation of the rules, there are plenty of options to consider. Once the style is set, follow it through with enthusiasm.

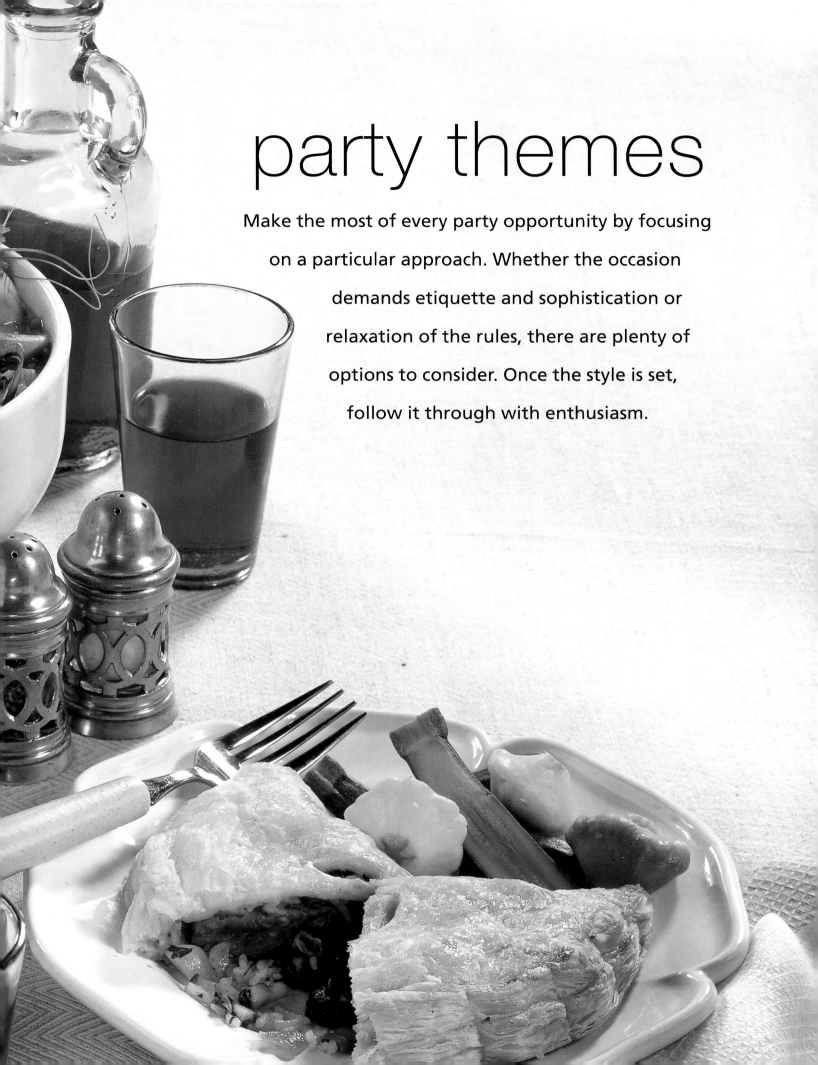

Shaken and Stirred: the Drinks Party

Today's drinks party is a celebration of relaxed sophistication. From easy evenings with friends to an opportunity for semi-formal pre- or post-wedding congratulations, sharing drinks and nibbles is sociable. Plan carefully to ensure the occasion flows smoothly.

Setting the scene

Try the following checklist for straightforward drinks party planning. Make lists of all your ideas while you write shopping lists and notes on aspects to organize.

• Define the occasion precisely.
• Focus on the ambience.
• Decide on the type of drinks.
• Select the style of finger food.

Occasion

Drinks party invitations range from "stylishly casual" to "lounge suit and tie" – a balance of relaxed formality in varying proportions. Within this context, define your occasion before making precise plans. For example, a wedding may provide the opportunity for a gathering of friends not invited to the ceremony and main meal, or a celebration with colleagues and

Below Colourful drinks add to the thrill of the cocktail hour.

business clients, neighbours or other associates outside your immediate circle of personal friends.

Whatever the occasion, the number of guests and whether you intend inviting one or more groups of people are important. There is no reason why a drinks party should be connected to any particular event – this is precisely the sort of opportunity to catch up with friends or meet and greet acquaintances. The party may be short – lunchtime or pre-dinner – or an open-ended evening. So there is plenty of scope for setting subtle differences in ambience once you have clear aims.

Drinks

Decide on the type of drinks: cocktails, champagne, wine or an open bar. Cocktails are classic pre-dinner drinks. Champagne is always acceptable and perfect when there is a special toast to raise. Red and white wines are a popular choice. Providing an open bar (that is, offering a selection of shorts and mixers, wine or beer) is the most difficult and expensive, but this can be successful for a limited number of guests, especially if you know them well. Always provide mineral water and a good choice of soft drinks as alternatives to alcohol.

Food style

The food should fit the occasion, ambience and drinks. A plentiful supply of chunky and satisfying finger food is ideal for the sort of relaxed drinks party that drifts into late evening. Dainty canapés and cocktail nibbles are sufficient for a short pre-dinner party. Generous quantities of extra-special, stylish finger food go down well on special occasions. Among the myriad of food options, remember bread and cheese; hot fondues and dips; or international savouries, such as Japanese sushi or Spanish tapas.

Above Arrange nibbles on platters so that guests can easily help themselves.

Serving snacks

Distribute plates or bowls of snacks around side tables and surfaces (protect surfaces to avoid damage from spills). Offer nibbles as you mingle, or move them near groups of guests and encourage everyone to dip in. Take platters of hot canapés around or enlist the help of a friend or co-host.

Below Hire a range of different cocktail glasses for an authentic touch.

Above *Avocado-filled eggs make excellent little canapés.*

Right *A selection of canapés and light bites suitable for a drinks party.*

Planning finger food

For stylish refreshments, present a modest range of excellent items. Select a number of complementary types of food, including variety in colour, texture and flavour. The following examples show how to match crisp and smooth textures and different ingredients and dishes. Broaden the variety by including a range of sandwich, tart or pastry fillings or toppings. In addition to the main snacks, distribute bowls of good quality bought (or home-made) nibbles, such as roasted nuts, breadsticks and Chinese rice crackers.

• Mini open sandwiches, crisp short pastry tartlets, fruit and cheese savouries on sticks, and crudités with dips.

• Filo-wrapped savouries, bread-based canapés, filled salad vegetables, and smoked salmon and/or ham rolls.

• Bitesize pizza pieces, Spanish tortilla squares, miniature fish cakes, cheese or meat croquettes, and crudités.

• Miniature kebabs, fish goujons, dried fruit wrapped in prosciutto, walnuts sandwiched with cream cheese.

• Smoked salmon sandwiches, marinated mini-mozzarella cheese skewered with cherry tomatoes.

• Excellent chocolate truffles.

Making canapés

The trick to making impressive canapés without an army of experts is by adopting a conveyor-belt method.

Buy large square sandwich loaves of white, wholemeal (whole-wheat) or rye bread and leave them unwrapped at room temperature for a day. Trim off the crusts, and then cut each loaf lengthways into large, fairly thin slices. Spread with the chosen topping, such as a savoury butter, flavoured soft cheese, pâté or spread. For speed, use a topping that can be piped, rather than spread, such as soft cheese or creamy mixtures. The bases can be prepared to this stage a day ahead; cover with clear film (plastic wrap) and pack in a plastic bag. Cut into squares or fingers.

Arrange the canapés on serving platters and then add the garnishes. For efficiency, prepare a tray that can be added to the topped canapés quickly and easily.

Fuss-free options include: lumpfish roe, peeled cooked tiger prawns (shrimp), stuffed green olives, pecan nut halves, halved cherry tomatoes, halved canned artichoke hearts or peeled and halved cucumber slices.

Portions

The amount guests will eat depends on the time of day and length of the party. The following is a rough guide to the number of bitesize canapés or snacks to prepare for comparatively formal occasions. It is as well to be aware that the more relaxed and lively the gathering, the more people are likely to eat.

• Allow 5 items per person as an appetizer with drinks before a meal.

• Allow 10–12 items per person for an early evening drinks party (assuming that guests will be going on to dinner elsewhere).

• Allow 12–14 items per person for evening refreshments following a late lunch party, wedding breakfast or reception. (Remember to increase this when inviting additional guests in the evening who have not shared the main meal.)

• Allow 14–16 small items per person for light lunchtime or supper refreshments.

at a time, keeping the rest of the pastry covered with clear film (plastic wrap) to prevent it from drying and cracking. Brush with a little melted butter or olive oil, or a mixture of both. Cut the sheet widthways into 7.5cm/3in wide strips.

For fingers, place a little full-flavoured filling across one end of a pastry strip. Fold the end and sides of the strip over, and then roll it up. To make triangles, place a little mound of filling in the middle of the strip about 4cm/1½in from the end. Fold the corner of the pastry and filling over into a triangle across one end, then continue folding the triangle of filling over along the length of the strip.

Perfect pastries

These can be prepared in advance; they are easy to eat, satisfying and versatile. Try the following tips for streamlined preparation:

Puff pastries: prepare three different full-flavoured, well-seasoned cooked fillings. For speedy preparation make squares, triangles and oblong shapes.

Brush the rolled-out pastry lightly with beaten egg before cutting it into 6cm/2½in squares. These can be paired to make square pastries or folded in half into triangles or oblongs. Use one filling for each shape and place a small mound in the appropriate place on

Below *Flaky filo fingers are easy to make for large numbers.*

Above *Little filled pastries are always popular party foods.*

each square – centre slightly generous amounts for squares (leave an equal number blank for topping); in one corner for triangles; and to one side for oblongs. Top the squares and fold the others in half. Press the edges together and place on baking sheets. Brush with beaten egg and bake at 220°C/425°F/ Gas 7 for 7–10 minutes, until well puffed and golden. Cool on wire racks.

Flaky filo savouries: filo pastry triangles or fingers are extremely easy and quick to make. Work on one sheet

Below *Individual tartlets make a substantial snack.*

Kebabs and cocktail-stick snacks

For party finger food, make kebabs and snacks on sticks that are super tasty and neat:

• Thread no more than three miniature items on mini-kebabs.

• Cook trays of marinated ingredients, such as chicken or beef, then cool and thread them on to mini-wooden skewers. Reheat on ovenproof serving platters. Try cubes of chicken or gammon, mini-meatballs, mini-sausages, slices of spicy sausage, squares of (bell) pepper, small pickling onions, halved baby aubergines (eggplants) or cherry tomatoes.

Below *Soft cheese, herbs and nuts make a great pastry filling.*

Filling ideas for pastries

• Mash a 50g/2oz can of sardines in olive oil with the oil from the can, 1 crushed garlic clove, 2 finely chopped spring onions (scallions), the grated rind of 1 lemon, a squeeze of lemon juice, salt and a pinch of chilli powder.

• Mix finely chopped or minced (ground) cooked ham with a little freshly grated Pecorino cheese, a generous dollop of wholegrain mustard and plenty of chopped fresh chives.

• Mix plenty of finely chopped sun-dried tomatoes, pine nuts, a few chopped raisins and a generous pinch of dried oregano into cream cheese.

• Mash feta cheese to fine bread-crumbs and mix with chopped spring onion, a little oregano and enough ricotta cheese to bind the mixture into a paste.

• Mix chopped, well-drained cooked spinach with chopped spring onion, 1 chopped garlic clove (optional), a little freshly grated Parmesan cheese and enough ricotta to make a firm paste. Season with salt, pepper and a little nutmeg.

• Make sure cocktail-stick (toothpick) bites are bitesize rather than too large to pop into the mouth in one go. (Biting savouries off sticks can mean that the piece left on the stick falls off.)

• Strips of tender foods that roll well are good spread with soft cheese or used as wrappers for firm ingredients. Roll smoked halibut or salmon, cured or cooked ham, salami, peeled roasted (bell) peppers or canned pimientos.

• Olives, melon balls, halved cooked baby new potatoes, cubes of

Above *Many supermarkets now sell good-quality prepared sushi.*

cucumber, pieces of dried fruit (prunes, apricots or dates) and radishes are tasty wrapped in cooked or cured meat.

Simply stylish sushi

Sushi is delicious and practical as it can be prepared ahead, arranged on platters, covered and chilled. Ideally, make the sushi a few hours in advance; however, it can be prepared the day before. Keep it well wrapped to prevent the rice from hardening. Remove from the refrigerator about 30 minutes before serving.

• Rolled sushi: buy mini-sheets of toasted and seasoned nori seaweed to make cocktail-sized rolled sushi rice. Top with dressed cooked sushi rice and add two or three strips of ingredients such as cucumber, spring onion (scallion), cooked carrot or cooked dried shiitake mushrooms marinated in soy sauce and a little sherry. Roll up firmly and neatly. Wrap each roll in clear fim (plastic wrap), twisting the ends firmly. Cut into small pieces before serving.

• Mini-moulded sushi: shape mini-sushi squares by pressing the dressed, cooked rice into ice cube trays. Place a small square of smoked salmon, smoked halibut, thin omelette or thinly sliced smoked or marinated tofu in the bottom of each ice cube compartment before pressing in the rice and topping each one with another square of the same or a piece of nori. Unmould on to a board and top with a suitable garnish, such as lumpfish roe, quartered cucumber slices and/or pieces of pickled ginger. Serve with small bowls of wasabi or light soy dipping sauce.

Below *A big mixed salad is almost a meal in itself.*

Fabulous Fork Food

Formal or casual, this type of food is fun to prepare, simple to serve and effortless to eat. Make light of the planning by adopting a completely practical approach to this style of buffet instead of stretching it beyond its limits.

Menu options

The fork buffet menu may be for a two- or three-course meal, laid out in stages, or a series of complementary refreshments presented together. Display a menu to let guests know what to expect and to encourage self-service. Although food must be complementary and marry well to form a meal if that is the intention, a party buffet is an occasional treat, so well-balanced nutritional value is not necessarily a priority.

Below Cut large tarts into slices so that they are easy to eat with just a fork.

When offering a first course, serve it from a separate side table before placing main dishes on the buffet to avoid any confusion over what should be eaten first. When serving a comparatively small number (10–20 guests) it may be easier to present the first course served on small plates, with accompanying cutlery. These can be arranged on a side table or handed around from trays.

For a stylish main course, focus on one or two main dishes and add easy-to-eat main accompaniments, such as creamy mashed potatoes, rice, pasta or couscous. To avoid overflowing plates, limit the number of vegetable or salad accompaniments to one or two that really make the most of the main dish.

When serving a range of savoury refreshments rather than a traditionally well-balanced main course, select dishes that are contrasting rather than complementary. However, avoid

Above *Individual vegetable terrines are light, elegant fork food.*

clashing flavours as guests often sample a little of each dish instead of eating just one or two.

Desserts are not likely to be confused with the main course, so they can be arranged towards the back of the buffet table to be moved forward when the main dishes have been cleared away.

Cheese can be seen as an alternative to main dishes, so if you want it strictly as a separate course, set the cheese board and accompaniments on a side table away from the main buffet.

Practical fork food

There is nothing worse than doing battle with food that is difficult to eat while balancing a glass and trying to make conversation.

• Serve ingredients in small pieces or that can be broken easily with the side of a fork.
• Select foods and dishes that cling together well and are easily scooped up on a fork.
• While moist dishes are successful, excess thin sauce can be difficult to eat and will drip easily.
• Match dishes or ingredients with complementary sauces or dressings

Above *Stuffed vine leaves can be home-made or bought from the deli.*

rather than serving a main dish and accompaniments in different sauces that clash or are too runny.

Favourite foods

The following dishes are always popular and are easy to serve:
• Baked pasta dishes, such as lasagne and cannelloni. Try fillings with seafood, poultry, vegetable or ricotta cheese as alternatives to meat.
• Dishes full of bitesize chunks in lightly thickened sauces – lamb or chicken curries, boeuf à la bourguignonne, beef casseroles, coq au vin made with boneless chunks of chicken, ratatouille.
• Comforting mince (ground beef) dishes – chilli con carne, moussaka and bitesize meatballs in tomato sauce.
• Moreish rice dishes, such as creamy risotto, slightly spicy kedgeree and rice

salad with a fine yet light, slightly creamy dressing.
• Creamy potato salad, fine-cut coleslaw, tomato and mozzarella salad made with halved cherry tomatoes.

Below *Savoury rice dishes are easily eaten with just a fork.*

Stylish options

Add one or two stylish variations to a fork supper. Try one of the following:
• Savoury moulds and creamy mousses, such as seafood or vegetable terrines, fish or seafood mousses, tender foods or eggs in aspic.
• Dressed salmon, Coquille St. Jacques or other seafood gratins.
• International specialities such as a saffron risotto with shredded Parma ham and basil, seafood paella or spicy Moroccan-style tagine.

Desserts

These are often overlooked for informal fork buffets: this is unfortunate because their are plenty of options. Individual pots or dishes are easy to eat but they do take up space. Large items and big bowls that cut easily or can be spooned out are most practical.
• Fruit salads, mousses and fools.
• Filo pastries with soft cheese, nut, fruit or chocolate fillings.
• Superlative trifle, light-as-air meringues, luscious chocolate desserts.
• Miniature portions of desserts, such as cheesecake, individual gâteaux, bitesize shortcake or tiny fruit tarts.

Below *Fresh feta cheese, good quality olives and bread are excellent party fare.*

Dinner from the **Buffet**

Balance dinner-party formality with self-service simplicity by offering a traditional menu buffet style. This is an excellent way of sharing a special meal with a larger number of guests than you would normally want to invite to dinner. The ambience can be stylish, with attractively garnished food, elegant table settings and all the trimmings that make memorable celebrations, but without the need for close attention from host or hostess during the meal. A buffet is a good way to entertain whether in a hired room or in a marquee erected at home.

Table tips

Lay out a buffet table to one side of the dining room or in a separate area – this may be another adjacent room, hallway or dining area within the kitchen. Prepare a separate side table for dessert, if necessary, and have the cheese course set out ready for self-service or to be taken to the table when appropriate. Allow room for guests to walk past the buffet without disrupting others seated at the table. Plan the "flow" of guests, arranging food to encourage logical movement in one direction. Prepare a discreet table, trolley or area on which to deposit used plates from the first and main courses, remembering to include a suitable container to take cutlery.

Set the dining table or several different dining tables – a conservatory, hallway or patio can be used instead of, or as well as, the usual dining area. When preparing several tables, take care to arrange them so that they are linked without any one being isolated.

Select a cold first course that can be plated and placed on the tables before guests sit down. Have table heaters, if necessary, for hot main-course dishes, so that they can be arranged on the buffet before guests sit down to the appetizer.

Simple dishes ensure success

The food does not have to be fork friendly – everyone will be sitting down to eat – but it should be approachable for self-service.

• A main course made up of individual portions looks neat and attractive, and

Below *Make sure there are plenty of napkins on or near the buffet table.*

Above *Choose a selection of dishes that are suitable for self-service.*

guests will not be intimidated by having to cut or carve. Individual pastries, fish steaks or rolled fillets, or chicken breast portions are typical.

• Casseroles made up of evenly cut ingredients are a good choice.

• Select dishes that can be kept hot successfully without spoiling. Sauced portions or wrapped ingredients that will not dry out easily are the best choices. Pan-fried or freshly grilled items that have to be served freshly cooked are best avoided.

• Instead of plain cooked vegetable accompaniments, select a gratin, purée, casserole or bake that will stay hot without spoiling.

• Bowls of refreshing complementary side salad can be placed on the dining table after the first course.

• Cold salsas, sauces or condiments for main dishes can be placed on the dining table.

• Platters of individual desserts look elegant and are easy to serve – try making individual versions of large recipes, such as little fruit tarts, mini-gâteaux, meringue pairs, little choux pastries and individual mousses or moulded sweets.

Menu reminders

Remember the usual rules for creating good menus: go for complementary flavours, contrasting textures and appealing colours. In addition, when serving the food buffet-style consider the following ideas:

• Easy appetizers: arrange stylish portions of salads that will not wilt on individual plates at the table. Try marinated roasted vegetables and mini or cubed cheese; cured meats with olives, Parmesan flakes and crusty bread; little cheese or vegetable mousses with crisp savoury biscuits (crackers); home-made fish or meat pâté with tiny dinner rolls; smoked salmon marinated with chopped fresh dill and mustard in olive oil; or pickled herring with shredded cooked beetroot (beet) and horseradish.

• Simple-to-serve main dishes: cubed boneless chicken or turkey breast; venison, beef, lamb or pork all make delicious casseroles enriched with wine and spirits; or cook breast fillets of chicken, turkey, pheasant or duck in wine sauces reduced to a thin glaze for coating. Cook boneless portions of fish, poultry or meat in filo or puff pastry, adding herb butter before wrapping. Game, poultry or vegetarian pies are suitable for formal and informal buffet meals, and whole cooked salmon is always popular.

• No-fuss accompaniments: simple leafy salads with dressings served on the side; creamy mashed potatoes flavoured with herbs, garlic, spring onions (scallions) and olives; roasted mixed vegetables dressed with citrus

Above *Whole meat joints can be carved and served at the buffet.*

rind and herbs after cooking; vegetable gratins; or casseroles of Mediterranean vegetables, such as ratatouille.

• So to dessert: for an elegant statement, make a simple salad of two or three fruits with an intriguing hint of additional flavour – try mango and raspberry dressed with orange juice and a little honey; strawberry and papaya with a hint of lime rind and

Above *Home-made truffles make a wonderful finishing touch to any party.*

juice; chilled pears poached in cider with melon and chopped preserved stem ginger; or pineapple marinated with cardamom and sprinkled with coconut. Classic individual dishes, such as crème caramel or crème brûlée and meringue nests, are all good for a buffet.

Below *Contrasting colours and textures provide an appetizing display.*

Dinner Party Planner

Many dinner parties may be sheer fun, others sedate and some involve a sense of duty but all should be sociable and stylish. Achieving the latter ultimate goal does mean putting in a little forethought and planning – but do not be daunted, entertaining is the most rewarding part of greeting and meeting. Ultimately, dinner parties should be enjoyable.

Style guide

Hitting the high point means making a few well-calculated plans:
• Scour the guest list for flaws to be sure of surrounding the table with people who will amuse each other (even if they don't entirely agree).
• Adopt a definite approach to ambience: relaxed businesslike, society smart, well-acquainted casual, lively and up-beat, socially sexy, friendly calm, or intimate.

Below *A rack of lamb is impressive for a formal dinner.*

Above *Home-made rolls add a special touch to a dinner party.*

• Plan the menu, table décor, room trimmings and lighting, background music, pre- and post-dinner nibbles and petits fours to fit in with the required ambience.
• Check out linen, crockery, cutlery and serving dishes in advance.
• Ensure cloakroom and other areas open to guests fit in with the ambience.

Above *Lobster claws make an unusual garnish for soup.*

• Be sure to allow time for spring cleaning – or organize cleaners to do so for you – a few days beforehand and last-minute tidying up.

Menu impressions

Effortless catering is always the most impressive. As a guest, there is nothing worse than acting as spectator to the host's or hostess's insecurities and kitchen inadequacies. Keep it simple and do not attempt anything out of your league.
• Check guests' diets beforehand if you do not know them well – just ring and ask if there is anything they do not eat.
• Plan a practical menu, with the majority of dishes ready in advance and requiring little last-minute attention.
• Buy the best ingredients you can afford and use simple methods.
• Use familiar recipes or try out new ones beforehand.

Planning and timing

From the menu, make a shopping list and then a list of "things to do" in the order in which they have to be done. Make sure you double check that you have included everything:
• Pre-dinner drinks and nibbles.
• Appetizer and bread.

- Fish or soup course.
- Sorbet (sherbet) to cleanse the palate.
- Main course.
- Vegetables and side salads.
- Dessert and biscuits (cookies).
- Cheese board and crackers.
- Coffee and chocolates or petits fours.
- Wine for each course, water and after-dinner drinks.

You may not want to include everything from this definitive list, but make a note of what has to be done and by when. If there is too much to do on the day or at the last minute, change some of the dishes to cook-ahead items or reduce the number of courses. Pre-plan shopping, cooking, serving and clearing up as you go along. Remember to allow time for relaxation and getting yourself in the mood well before guests arrive.

Quantity guide
The following is a rough guide when serving 4–8 people. The quantities vary according to the number of courses and type of dishes, but the amounts give some idea of the portions that "look" generous without being daunting. As numbers increase over about ten, the amounts per person

Below *Asparagus in season can make any dish special.*

tend to go down (except for individual items). You may well be preparing a multi-course menu with small portions for each course or you may know that guests have modest appetites.

When inviting people you do not know well, the solution is to opt for pre-portioned foods that you can count out per person and to prepare generous amounts of vegetables and salads rather than risk running out.

Appetizers, per portion:
- 250ml/8fl oz/1 cup soup.
- 75g/3oz shellfish or 115g/4oz prepared fish.
- 25g/1oz salad leaves (such as watercress or lettuce).

Main course:
- 175g/6oz prepared fish, 1 fish steak or 1 small whole fish per portion.
- 175–225g/6–8oz portion of poultry or meat or 1 modest poultry or game breast fillet per portion.
- 225g/8oz poultry, game or meat for casseroles per portion.
- 1 roast duck serves two to three.
- 1 roast pheasant serves two.
- 1 small game bird per portion.

Above *Simple meat and vegetables can be beautifully presented.*

Accompaniments, per portion:
- 75g/3oz vegetables such as beans, peas, broccoli and carrots, or salad.
- 1 baked potato.
- 3–5 boiled new potatoes.
- 2–3 roast potatoes.
- 50g/2oz uncooked rice.
- 75–115g/3–4oz uncooked pasta.
- 2–3 thick slices of crusty white or wholemeal (whole-wheat) bread.

Below *Frozen soufflés are perfect for preparing in advance.*

Fondue Flair

Although the fondue drifts in and out of fashion, it is always enjoyable and definitely a hassle-free option for light-hearted social gatherings. Serving fondue involves the minimum of time-consuming cooking, provides entertaining dining and allows guests to participate in the cooking process and select and sample as much or as little as they wish.

Fondue style

The following styles of fondue are open to interpretation and variation to create a variety of different menus:
• Classic Swiss-style cheese fondue is fabulously creamy with crusty bread and crisp vegetables or fruit.
• Fondue Bourguignonne consists of cubes of lean tender steak cooked in a pot of hot oil, and then eaten with accompanying sauces. Poultry and other meats are also cooked this way.

Fondue etiquette

Long-handled forks with different coloured ends (for identification) are used to dip ingredients into the fondue pot. Forgetting the colour of your fork is greatly frowned upon, as is leaving ingredients to cook in the pot for too long. When someone drops a piece of food off the fork into the pot, they are traditionally expected to kiss the other diners of the opposite sex!

Above *Garlic croûtes make a change from the cubes of bread that are traditionally dipped into a Swiss cheese fondue.*

• Fondue Chinois is an interpretation of the Mongolian firepot method of cooking a mixture of raw ingredients in simmering broth. Seafood, marinated chicken, little Chinese-style dumplings (dim sum) and vegetables are lowered into the broth, and then scooped out in miniature baskets. The wonderful broth is the final treat of the meal, usually with added vegetables, noodles or other ingredients simmered briefly before it is served.
• Dessert fondues are sweet dips served with pieces of fruit, finger biscuits (cookies) or cake for dipping. Chocolate fondues can be dark (bitter-sweet) or luscious with white chocolate and cream. Warm, thick fruit fondues laced with liqueur are perfect with mini-sponge cakes or cubes of brioche.

Dip and dine

Cheese fondue is simple to make and effortless to eat. Depending on the ingredients and accompaniments, it fits well into the simplest or most sophisticated dinner party setting.

Buy good quality crusty baguette early on the day or a day ahead, so that it is slightly stale, and cut it into bitesize chunks for dipping. Chunks of celery, fennel and apple also go well with cheese fondue. Firm, ripe cherry tomatoes and large juicy seedless grapes are easy to dip and delicious with a robust fondue.

Below *Croûtons make bitesize dippers, but slices of fresh bread are good too.*

Above *Always use long-handled forks to cook your food.*

Any other accompaniments should be simple – a crisp, refreshing side salad of leaves and herb sprigs clears the palate perfectly. Little new potatoes drizzled with a hint of good olive or walnut oil and sprinkled with chives balance the rich cheese, as does a simple salad of tomato strewn with finely chopped red onion.

Fondue sets
Sets are available that incorporate a pot, stand, forks and a burner. Cheaper sets with just a rack and burner can also be bought, as can individual pots and pans, forks and skewers.

Cutlery
Dinner forks can be used for dipping food into a fondue. However, when cooking food in the fondue, forks with wooden handles are needed, as the metal of a fork or skewer will get hot when left in the fondue. Small wire baskets can be used to fish out food that has been deep-fried or cooked in stock. Chopsticks or wooden tongs are the authentic equipment for cooking sukiyaki and tempura. For dipping, food can also be speared onto skewers.

Simple cheese fondue
For the simplest cheese fondue, the basic proportions to serve four as a main course (with accompaniments) are 500g/1¼lb cheese to 250ml/ 8fl oz/1 cup wine. The finished fondue should have a creamy consistency.

For a fabulous fondue, gently heat 1 halved garlic clove, 1 thin slice of onion, 1 blade of mace and 1 large bay leaf in 150ml/¼ pint/⅔ cup dry or medium-dry white wine until just simmering. Cover and set aside for several hours or overnight. Finely grate 225g/8oz each of Gruyère and Emmenthal cheese and 25g/1oz fresh Parmesan. Place the cheeses in a large bowl and thoroughly but lightly mix in 30ml/2 tbsp plain (all-purpose) flour with a little freshly ground black pepper until the cheese is evenly coated. (Take care not to compact the grated cheese into clumps or it will not melt as easily.)

Strain the wine into a heavy fondue pan and heat until boiling. Reduce the heat to low, so that the wine is kept hot but off the boil, and immediately begin to stir in handfuls of floured cheese. After adding a couple of handfuls, allow the cheese to melt before adding more. Continue adding the cheese, melting it gently and stirring constantly. Finally, add 45ml/ 3 tbsp Kirsch and bring to the boil, stirring, until the fondue is smooth and slightly thickened. Add salt and ground black pepper, if required, and a little freshly grated nutmeg. Transfer the pan to a spirit burner at the table and regulate the flame to keep the fondue hot but not boiling.

Alternative cheeses
Dolcelatte makes a creamy blue cheese fondue when used half and half with Gruyère. For blue cheese fondue that bites back, use Gorgonzola, Bleu d'Auvergne or Roquefort. Pep up blue cheese fondues with brandy instead of Kirsch.
• Other suitable cheeses include Beaufort, mozzarella, Edam, Fontina and Cheddar; try them for their subtle differences of taste and texture.
• For an economical choice, opt for mature (sharp) Cheddar and dry cider. Add a generous dollop of wholegrain mustard and omit the Kirsch.

Below *Classic Swiss cheese fondue with baby vegetables.*

Fondue Bourguignonne

This dish demands the finest beef and perfect condiments. Complementary side salads and warm crusty bread are the traditional accompaniments. Bring the beef to life with an imaginative mixed green salad, such as lightly dressed fine green beans on a bed of peppery rocket (arugula) and sprinkled with shredded basil, or try finely shredded fennel, celery and (bell) peppers on a generous base of rocket, watercress or salad leaves. Baked potatoes topped with sour cream, or crisp new potatoes roasted in their skins also taste terrific with the beef.

The choice of condiments and sauces can set the style for fondue Bourguignonne: they can be simple to prepare, such as a sophisticated béarnaise sauce or mayonnaise flavoured with garlic, chopped herbs, mustard or tomato. Chutneys, relishes, gherkins, pickled dill cucumbers and finely chopped onion are often served, and barbecue sauce is sometimes

Below *Spicy potato wedges go well with a creamy fondue.*

offered. Slightly spicy fresh tomato salsa or herby green salsa contribute a lighter feel.

Allow 175–225g/6–8oz good quality fillet or rump steak per portion. Trim off all the fat and cut it into 2cm/¾ in cubes. Arrange the steak on small individual plates. Individual bowls of condiments and sauces are a good idea or large bowls can be passed around the table. Whatever the choice, the accompaniments can be prepared and chilled in advance.

Heat oil in the fondue pan on the stove, and then place it on the spirit burner at the table to keep it hot for cooking the meat. Remind guests that their forks are hot and the cooked meat should be scraped off for eating.

Fondue Chinois

This is quite different and light. The quality of stock is vital, so make it with 450g/1lb lean pork, 1 chicken leg and thigh quarter, 1 quartered large onion, 4 spring onions (scallions), 2 slices of fresh root ginger, 2 garlic cloves, a few sprigs of fresh coriander (cilantro) leaves and 1 lemon grass stalk or a strip

Above *Crunchy vegetables perfectly complement a savoury fondue.*

of pared lemon rind. Place in a large pan, cover with cold water and bring to the boil. Skim the stock, then reduce the heat and cover the pan. Leave the stock to simmer very gently for 1½ hours. Strain and season lightly.

To serve the broth: when all the ingredients have been cooked, taste the broth, which will be concentrated by this stage. Dilute the broth to taste with boiling water or adjust the seasoning and add some shredded spring onions and greens. Simmer the soup for a few minutes before ladling it into bowls.

Safety notes

- If oil is overheated it could burst into flames. If it catches light, carefully place a lid or a large plate over the top of the pan to cut off the air supply. Never pour water on to burning oil.
- Make sure that the food for dipping is dry, as wet food will cause the oil to spit.
- Protect your hands when moving a hot pan.
- Check that the fondue pot is secure on its stand on the table and that it cannot be knocked over accidentally.
- Never leave a lighted burner or candle unattended.

Above *Biscotti, small fruits and cakes are wonderful with sweet fondues.*

Right *Crab cakes cooked in oil with a chunky, spicy cucumber relish.*

Ingredients to cook

Prepare a selection of ingredients to cook in oil or stock – remember that dumplings for simmering can be bought from specialist stores. Try peeled raw tiger prawns (shrimp), scallops, cubes of chicken breast fillet or pork, pork meatballs flavoured with sesame, ginger and garlic, dim sum, tofu and

Below *Crème Anglaise with raspberry meringue and summer fruits.*

vegetables such as mustard greens or Chinese leaves. The ingredients can be marinated separately with aromatics or seasonings, such as soy sauce, five-spice powder, shredded ginger, spring onions or chopped garlic.

Dipping sauces and accompaniments

Whether plain or marinated, the cooked ingredients are dipped in a little sauce before they are eaten. Provide individual dishes of dipping sauce for each diner. A mixture of soy sauce and dry sherry, with a drop of sesame oil, a little finely shredded spring onion and finely chopped garlic is powerful and delicious. Plain soy sauce, hoisin sauce or plum sauce also make good dips.

Shredded vegetables, such as cucumber, spring onions and Chinese leaves, are refreshing accompaniments, and plain boiled or steamed rice completes the meal.

Sweet fondues

• Some fruits, such as grapes and apples, are suitable for dipping into savoury as well as sweet fondues. Take advantage of fruits in season for sweet fondues: strawberries, cherries, plums, peaches, apricots and nectarines are all suitable, as well as exotic fruits such as figs, pineapple, papaya, mangoes, star fruit and lychees. Fruits available all year, such as bananas and the citrus fruits, also dip well. Underripe fruit can be lightly poached in sugar syrup, fruit juice or a fruity wine.

• Cakes, biscuits and cookies: slices of dense-textured cake and sweet biscuits or cookies make excellent dippers for sweet fondues. Try Madeira cake, meringues, biscotti or Danish pastries.

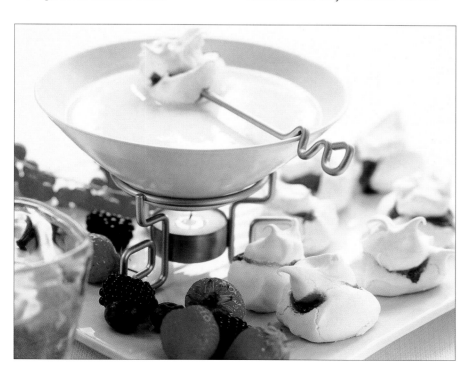

Brunches and Lunches

Parties between mid-morning and mid-afternoon range from laid-back indulgence time to lively and invigorating gatherings, from sophisticated low-key relaxation to fun with friends.

Dining and sharing

Brunch or lunch is often closely linked to shared activities, such as family excursions, sport or shopping; they may be part of a weekend house party; or a follow-on with overnight dinner or party guests. Food should be inconspicuously successful rather than dominating on these occasions, which calls for well-planned and completely practical menus. Prepare ahead or serve the easiest cook-and-share dishes; creative deli shopping is the clever choice.

Cook-ahead options include large or individual quiches, such as classic quiche Lorraine; set omelettes, such as Italian-style frittata or Spanish tortilla that can be served hot or cold; and chunky soups. Sweet breads, muffins and fruit compotes or salads are all good cook-ahead items. Refresh baked goods briefly in the oven before serving. Cook-and-share dishes are ideal for kitchen gatherings, when

Below *Keep family and informal entertaining relaxed by using simple napery, crockery and cutlery.*

guests congregate to help cook and serve and then eat in an informal atmosphere. Pancakes or waffles are ideal for eating over a long, relaxed joint cooking session. Egg dishes, such as fluffy omelettes or scrambled eggs, are also good options for sociable cook-together brunches.

Self-assembly open sandwiches are ideal for kitchen lunches – just lay out all the prepared ingredients and breads for guests to help themselves. For relaxed success, have all breads, ingredients and accompaniments prepared and laid out in platters, bowls and baskets.

Creative deli shopping makes a superbly simple meal. For menu sense and stylish presentation, focus on one type of food or, for larger gatherings, keep different types of ingredients separate. Display a selection of different salami and cured raw meats, such as prosciutto and bresaola, on a large platter. Arrange cooked or smoked poultry and meat on another tray, and seafood and smoked fish together. Present cheeses on a board. Garnish each platter lightly with herbs and wedges of citrus fruit. Provide olive oil for drizzling over.

Include dried and fresh fruit, pickles and breads to complement the savoury platters. Croissants, bagels and mixed breads can be served with savoury as well as sweet foods; brioches, sweet breads and fruit buns go with fruit conserves, marmalade, honey or maple syrup. Sour cream, fromage frais or cream cheese go well with savoury or sweet ingredients, including smoked salmon or croissants with fruit conserve.

Summertime chill-out

Light foods are ideal for relaxed brunches or lunches in the sun. Offer warm crusty bread, light rye bread, mini-rolls, croissants or thinly sliced bread and butter as accompaniments.

Above *Fish chowders are excellent for winter lunches and brunches.*

Below *American pancakes with crisp bacon make a tasty brunch dish.*

Below *Chive scrambled eggs in brioches are the ultimate brunch treat.*

Above *Iced melon soup with mint sorbet is a refreshing summer dish.*

Include one, two or more courses, or just set out an array of foods in a cool kitchen for everyone to wander and sample as they please, such as:

• Chilled fruit soups, lively citrus sorbets (sherbets) or fresh fruit salads are stylish and refreshing. Alternatively, serve prepared exotic fruit, melons and berries on a bed of ice.

• Muesli ingredients are satisfying with fruit – oat, barley and rye flakes, nuts, seeds and dried fruit can be mixed or served in separate bowls. Offer honey, maple syrup, yogurt and milk for moistening the fruit and grains.

• Offer simple grilled (broiled) seafood – lobster, large prawns (shrimp), scallops or oysters – dressed with butter and served with lemon.

• Summer dishes, such as dressed salmon, chicken salads or baked ham, are good cook-ahead main dishes.

• Asparagus or globe artichokes are a treat with melted butter and lemon.

Winter indulgence

Cold weather is the time for lingering over several courses of favourite foods and dishes.

• Serve warm compotes of dried fruit lightly spiced with cinnamon and cloves.

• Simmer porridge slowly, then serve it with brown sugar and extra cream.

• Opt for an indulgent cooked breakfast, with gloriously aromatic grilled bacon, sausages, kidneys, tomatoes and crisp fried bread. Fried potatoes or potato pancakes and poached or fried eggs are essential.

• Poached kippers or smoked haddock are delicious with poached eggs, and buttered, lightly cooked spinach.

• Serve pats of butter creamed with chopped parsley and grated lemon rind to dress plain cooked eggs – baked, poached or boiled. Creamy scrambled eggs are special when served with smoked salmon.

• Remember to round off winter breakfasts with warm fresh American muffins or toasted English muffins with butter and marmalade.

House-guest breakfasts and brunches

A take-it-or-leave-it kitchen buffet of fresh fruits, yogurt, cereals and warm breakfast breads provides an informal and successful start to the day. This can be extended to include sophisticated cold platters or cooked dishes.

• Wake-up trays of tea or coffee and biscuits or cookies in the bedroom provide welcome refreshment.

• Prepare cook-ahead dishes to avoid early morning work before guests rise.

• Set the breakfast table or prepare everything last thing the night before, after guests have retired, if possible, so that you can relax in the morning.

Lingering over a roast lunch

The great British tradition of Sunday roast lunch with all the trimmings is still comforting in cool weather. Start by serving a tray of little canapés or nibbles with pre-lunch drinks – offer small quantities of tiny smoked salmon sandwiches, salted nuts and pretzels. Serve a small portion of smooth, light soup as a first course. Then cleanse the palate with a melon or citrus fruit cocktail or a small portion of sorbet. For the main course, try the following traditional combinations:

• Rib of beef with Yorkshire pudding, roast and boiled potatoes, roast parsnips, buttered carrots, crisp, lightly cooked cabbage, rich port-reduced cooking jus, horseradish sauce and wholegrain mustard.

• Leg of lamb with new potatoes, baby carrots in tarragon butter, fine green beans, red-wine cooking jus, mint sauce and redcurrant jelly.

• Shoulder of pork with crisp crackling, roast potatoes, sage and onion stuffing, stir-fried red cabbage with raisins, creamy mashed swede (rutabaga), apple sauce and gravy.

• Chicken with parsley and thyme stuffing, salad or new potatoes roasted in their skins, roasted carrot wedges, crunchy broccoli, lightly cooked spinach and bread sauce.

• Desserts can be traditional favourites, such as fruit pies or crumbles and custard, or baked rice pudding with a poached fruit compote, or lighter alternatives, including crème caramel, fruit salad or a light mousse, chilled soufflé or creamy cheesecake.

Below *Succulent roast rib of beef cooked to perfection, served with horseradish, is a Sunday lunch treat.*

Children's Parties

Setting the scene for children's parties is enormous fun. Selecting a favourite character and using bought stationery and decorations is comparatively quick but it can be expensive. Picking an individual theme is more flexible and it can be based on anything from a popular figure to a favourite subject.

Below *Young guests will feel special with individual place name cards.*

Fun themes

The following are a few ideas to use as the basis for designing – or buying – invitations, goodie bags, decorations and games. They can be used as a theme for fancy dress or making masks, as well as on stationery and decorations. Draw simple images in bold black pen (or use a computer) and copy or print to make cut-out decorations to hang on the wall or stick on the corners of the table. Paint splashes of colour on the copies and add glitter. The birthday cake and novelty foods, such as cut-out cookies and sandwiches, should also match.
• Clowns – you could also hire a juggler to teach the young clowns.
• Pirates – a good theme for a treasure hunt; make sure everyone has a loot bag to take home.
• Witches and wizards – enlist a magician to add a little magic.

Above *A children's party is an ideal opportunity to create a bright table.*

• Dragons and monsters – friendly or fierce, hire a musician for musical participation and entertainment on the theme or set up a monster karaoke session.

Below *Sugar mice in bright colours will go down a treat with youngsters.*

Above *Decorate home-made letter cookies with pretty ribbon.*

• Wild animals – a great theme for hiring a face-painting entertainer or enlisting the help of a few willing adults to paint young faces.
• Balloons – use the balloon theme for decoration and fancy dress, and hire a balloon modeller to keep the youngsters entertained.
• Puppet party – have a hand puppet-making party and hire a puppet show.
• Girls' makeover – for little girls or teenagers, put together fun make-up kits and demonstrate a few beauty tips or persuade a gifted friend to help.

For a simpler party, all of these themes would work equally well combined with traditional party games, such as musical statues,

Below *Make simple place cards from coloured card cut-outs.*

musical bumps, pass the parcel, pin the tail on the donkey, simple Simon, sardines and hunt the thimble.

Table magic
Use disposable or wipe-clean table covers and disposable or shatterproof plates and tumblers with colourful drinking straws. Make a centrepiece of candies and sweets or floating balloons. Decorate plain paper tablecloths with colourful cut-outs on the party theme, sticking them firmly in place. Keep decorations towards the middle of the table so that they do not get in the way and cause more spills than necessary. Secure the table cover in place with sticky tape or ties so that it cannot be pulled to one side as little people jump off chairs.

It is better to have lots of small plates of food within easy reach than a few large platters. Have tuck boxes with bitesize foods ready at every place. Follow with little dishes of ice cream. Try a neat pyramid of fun little cakes instead of a big cake.

Small sweets
Children love sweet desserts, so opt for small portions of simple sweet dishes. Buy small colourful dessert containers for visual appeal.

Above *Bright plastic cups and crockery are practical for children's parties.*

• Fruit set in jelly is still a winner, especially with ice cream. Canned mandarin oranges, peaches or pineapple are all easy to eat. Halved or quartered fresh strawberries or whole fresh raspberries work well.
• Start ice cream sundaes in advance. Pile scoops of chocolate, strawberry and vanilla ice cream in dishes and keep them in the freezer. Add spoonfuls of prepared fruit and drizzle with chocolate or strawberry flavour sauce just before serving. Top with a whirl of whipped cream and a little iced cookie or jellied sweet (candy).

Below *Individual cup cakes can replace a large birthday or celebration cake.*

Barbecue Entertaining

Above *Serve small snacks that guests can nibble while the food is cooking.*

Below *Chargrilled pineapple with pineapple and chilli granita.*

Below *Sweet romano peppers stuffed with mozzarella cheese and olives.*

Achieving a relaxed atmosphere is the most important key to success for outdoor entertaining. The ultimate compliment guests can pay is being so at ease that they spontaneously become involved in cooking and serving at a barbecue. This *al fresco* impression of super-easy, impromptu entertaining is, in fact, usually the result of careful planning.

Barbecue food basics

The whole barbecue ambience is geared towards savouring the cooking process as well as the eating, so the menu should provide a relaxed first course that allows everyone to nibble while the main-course food items sizzle to perfection. For some occasions the idea of a main course of grilled food plus side dishes can be abandoned to a glorified sampling session. However, for the majority of occasions the following is a safe approach.

• An appetizer of dips, Italian-style antipasti or Greek-style meze works well. This may be finger food to nibble while standing around with drinks or trays of salads or marinated savouries to eat with bread at the table.

Above *Long, hot days herald the start of the barbecue season.*

• The main course can be grilled selected ingredients with planned accompaniments or a wider choice of "main" items and a range of side dishes. The latter can turn the whole barbecue into a relaxed and lengthy multi-course tasting session.
• It is a good idea to include fruit that can be grilled on the remains of the barbecue for dessert – bananas are terrific grilled in their skins and served with maple syrup and ice cream or cream; halved and stoned (pitted) peaches sprinkled with brown sugar and wrapped in foil can be cooked on the rack above dying embers; sliced fresh pineapple can be grilled on the barbecue or cooked in foil with rum and brown sugar; or marshmallows can be toasted on long forks.

Moreish morsels

Serve little dishes of the following to keep everyone happy while the barbecue heats and cooks the main course. Offer crusty bread and breadsticks with the savouries.

Above *Grilled bananas and ice cream are a classic barbecue dessert.*

• Mix thinly sliced garlic and chopped black olives with chopped fresh oregano and olive oil as a marinade for cubes of feta or mozzarella cheese.
• Halve baby plum tomatoes and toss with a little sugar, chopped red onion and plenty of chopped fresh mint. Drizzle with walnut oil.
• Buy plain canned rice-stuffed vine leaves and cut each one in half. Heat a crushed garlic clove with some dry white wine, plenty of olive oil, 2–4 bay leaves, a handful of pine nuts and a few fresh sage leaves. Bring to the boil, then remove from the heat and leave to cool before pouring over the halved stuffed vine leaves. Cover and chill for several hours or overnight. Sprinkle with lots of chopped fresh parsley and grated lemon rind before serving.
• Roast a mixture of baby carrots, pickling onions, turnips, radishes and chunks of red (bell) pepper together in olive oil in the oven until tender. Transfer to a serving dish, sprinkle with a dressing made from lemon juice, sugar, seasoning, a little mustard, capers and olive oil. Leave to cool and serve sprinkled with shredded fresh basil.
• Heat a few bay leaves and a handful of fennel seeds in olive oil in a large pan. Add cleaned button (white) or closed-cap mushrooms and season lightly. Cover and cook, stirring often, until the mushrooms have given up their liquid and are greatly reduced in size. Uncover and continue cooking until the liquor has evaporated, stirring occasionally. The mushrooms should be virtually dry and just beginning to sizzle in the remains of the olive oil. Transfer to a serving dish and drizzle with more olive oil. Leave to cool, then sprinkle with chopped parsley, a little chopped garlic and grated lemon rind. Serve with lemon wedges.

Bastes and glazes

Marinating is not essential but food should be brushed with oil, butter or another basting mixture to prevent it from drying out during grilling. The following can be brushed on foods during and after cooking.
• Olive oil flavoured with herbs, garlic, citrus rind or chillies.
• Dijon or wholegrain mustard diluted to a thin paste with sunflower or olive oil and sweetened with a little sugar.
• Equal quantities of tomato ketchup and wholegrain mustard mixed and thinned with a little sunflower oil.
• Sunflower oil flavoured and sweetened with clear honey and lemon or orange juice for a sharp contrast.
• A little tahini (sesame seed paste) stirred into natural (plain) yogurt, and

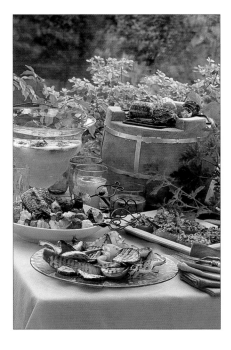

Above *Simple grilled vegetables make a delicious accompaniment.*

with a crushed garlic clove and finely chopped spring onion (scallion).
• Tomato purée (paste), a good pinch of sugar and a crushed garlic clove stirred into olive oil.
• The grated rind and juice of 1 lime mixed with natural yogurt with a pinch of dried red chillies, chopped fresh root ginger and chopped spring onion.

Below *Tongs are invaluable for turning and moving food over the hot coals.*

Marinating food

The point of marinating is to infuse flavour and moisten the food before grilling. Marinating also helps to tenderize meat. As a guide, a good marinade includes ingredients to keep the food moist during cooking – typically oil mixed with other liquid – aromatics and seasoning. Salt encourages moisture to seep from the food during marinating, so it is best to salt the food after marinating and just before grilling or partway through the cooking time.

• Always cool a hot marinade before pouring it over the food.

Grilling times

Cooking times are influenced by many factors, including the type of barbecue, heat of the coals, closeness of the cooking rack to the coals and thickness of food. All poultry, pork, sausages and burgers should be thoroughly cooked through. The following is a guide:

Total cooking time (turn items halfway through):
Fish steaks: 6–10 minutes
Small whole fish (sardines or small mackerel): 5–7 minutes
Large prawns (shrimp) in shells: 6–8 minutes
Chicken quarters: 30–35 minutes
Chicken drumsticks: 25–30 minutes
Boneless chicken breast fillet or turkey breast fillet: 10–15 minutes
Beef steaks (about 2.5cm/1in thick): 5–12 minutes (depending on required extent of cooking)
Burgers: 6–8 minutes
Lamb chops: 10–15 minutes
Pork chops: 15–18 minutes
Sausages: 8–10 minutes
Halved and seeded (bell) peppers: 5–8 minutes

• Keep food covered and cool during marinating – in the refrigerator if it is left for any more than an hour.
• Drain the food well before cooking and heat the marinade to boiling point in a small pan. Use this for basting food during cooking, then bring any leftover marinade to the boil and use it to glaze the food before serving. (Do not serve any remaining marinade from fish, meat or poultry without first boiling it as it will contain bacteria from the uncooked ingredients.)

Simple marinades

Lemon, thyme and caper marinade: for fish, seafood, poultry, gammon or game. Gently heat several sprigs of thyme in a little olive oil until they are just beginning to sizzle, then remove from the heat and add the grated rind and juice of 1 lemon. Whisk in freshly ground black pepper and some more oil, so that there is about twice the quantity of oil to lemon juice. Add 15ml/1 tbsp chopped capers and whisk well.

Orange, garlic and red wine marinade: this is good for all meats, game and red or green (bell) peppers. Peel a whole head of garlic and place the cloves in a small pan. Add 2 bay

Above *Fish brochettes with lime, lemon, garlic and olive oil marinade.*

leaves and 60ml/4 tbsp olive oil and cook gently for 5 minutes, stirring occasionally. Add the grated rind and juice of 1 orange, 5ml/1 tsp sugar, freshly ground black pepper and 300ml/½ pint/1¼ cups robust red wine. Bring to the boil and cook for about a minute, then remove from the heat and leave to cool before pouring over the ingredients to be marinated.

Mustard and rosemary marinade: a versatile marinade for oily fish, especially mackerel, and for poultry,

Below *Brush fish or meat frequently with a marinade during cooking to keep it moist.*

Above *Home-made beef or lamb burgers are popular dishes.*

meat, peppers, onions or mushrooms. Whisk 30ml/2 tbsp wholegrain mustard with 60ml/4 tbsp olive oil, 5ml/1 tsp sugar and pepper. Gently heat 250ml/ 8fl oz/1 cup dry white wine or dry (hard) cider with 3–4 fresh rosemary sprigs until boiling. Whisk into the mustard mixture and leave to cool before using.

Shortcuts for success
• Chicken joints, such as quarters and drumsticks, require lengthy cooking. For safety and speed when entertaining a crowd, pre-cook the portions in a covered roasting pan in the oven until just cooked but not well browned. Pour over a marinade or add seasoning. Cool and chill. Brown and thoroughly reheat the chicken on the barbecue.
• Potatoes take up lots of space, so pre-bake them in the oven until tender, then brush with oil and finish on the barbecue for crisp, well-flavoured skins.
• Boil small new potatoes in their skins until just tender, then toss with olive oil, a pinch of sugar, seasoning and a little mustard. Thread on metal skewers and grill until crisp and well browned.
• Grated potato pancakes are terrific on the barbecue. Make them in advance, cooking them until they are set but only very lightly browned. Cool, cover and chill. Grill on the barbecue until crisp and well browned.

Vegetarian barbecues
When cooking a mixed barbecue, organize a separate cooking area for vegetarian foods.
• Vegetables for marinating and grilling include halved and seeded peppers; slices or wedges of aubergine (eggplant); whole mushrooms; halved small beetroot (beet); par-boiled carrots; slices of butternut squash; halved courgettes (zucchini); blanched asparagus; and blanched fennel.
• For easy vegetable burgers, mix cooked and mashed carrots and potatoes, finely shredded white cabbage, chopped spring onions (scallions), finely chopped celery and chopped red pepper. Season, flavour with crushed garlic and shredded basil, then add enough fresh wholemeal (whole-wheat) breadcrumbs to bind the mixture firmly. Shape into burgers and brush with oil before grilling.
• Grill halved peppers cut sides down, remove them and fill with chopped fresh tomato, garlic and finely chopped fresh oregano, then grill skin sides down until well browned and tender. Serve topped with shavings of Parmesan cheese.

Food safety
• Keep food chilled until just before cooking.
• When serving food outside or keeping it ready for cooking, shade the table from the sun and cover food to keep insects off.
• Keep separate utensils for removing cooked fish, meat or poultry from the grill so as not to contaminate them with juices from raw or part-cooked items.
• Grill poultry and meat, and their products, high above the coals, or over medium heat, so that they cook through before becoming too brown outside.

• Marinate firm tofu with garlic and herbs in oil, then wrap in vine leaves and brush with oil for grilling.
• Marinate slices of firm halloumi cheese in olive oil with garlic and herbs, then grill until crisp and golden on both sides. Serve immediately.

Below *Langoustines are excellent barbecue food. Serve with mayonnaise.*

Packing up a **Picnic**

Individual adult hampers can be just as exciting and inventive as children's versions, especially when stylishly packed in extra-large linen napkins and tied into neat bundles. Try out a sample bundle, checking the amount and type of food it will hold and the number that can be stored in an insulated bag. Bundle contents can include portions of tasty cheese and charcuterie; small seeded rolls or baguettes, a small bowl of salad or marinated baby vegetables; and a little pot of condiment, salsa or dip. Individual bottles of champagne or wine can be included for a special touch.

Plan all the practical aspects of packing, transporting and consuming a picnic on separate lists compiled from menu requirements alongside the choice of food.

Picnic baskets are attractive and, while they are not the most practical choice for transporting food and equipment on large or informal family picnics, they are stylish for carrying china, cutlery and glassware for grand picnic meals. Lightweight crates that fit neatly into the storage area of a car are ideal for holding equipment. Wrap dishtowels and table linen around and between fragile items. Rigid plastic or disposable dishes, plastic cutlery and drinking containers can be stacked without fear of damage. Open baskets are light to carry and useful for bread.

Insulated bags keep food cool and in good condition. Soft bags are easy to carry and insulated backpacks are particularly practical when packing modest picnics. Although more awkward to carry, rigid chiller boxes protect delicate foods and bottles from damage as well as keeping food cool. Sort out or buy storage containers that stack neatly in chiller boxes to avoid tedious searching and shuffling when assembling the prepared picnic. Hi-tech

Above *A day beside the sea is an ideal opportunity for a summer picnic.*

storage boxes (designed for camping expeditions) can be plugged into the electrical supply of a car to act as a mini-refrigerator or as a modest oven for reheating food.

Relaxing in comfort
Folding chairs and tables may be *de rigueur* for flamboyant evening picnics but they are also comfortable for relaxed and informal meals. Decent chairs are far better than tiny, uncomfortable stools.

Rugs and cushions are a good choice. Damp-proof groundsheets or rugs with plastic backing are ideal. Pack umbrellas, sunshades and spare sun hats. Remember insect-repellent and storm candles.

Individual hampers
Children and adults alike love personal food packs and they are easy to prepare, distribute and eat. Colourful boxes that stack in a chiller bag can be filled with a selection of fun food packs. Drink packs can be packed separately and snack bags can contain fruit for a sweet course.

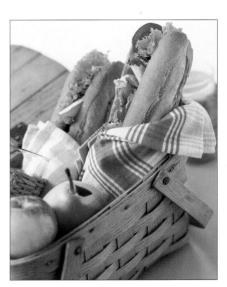

Above *Filled baguettes and fresh fruit form the basics of a tasty picnic.*

Below *Individual picnic packs are especially popular with children.*

Above *A wicker basket is practical when transporting bottles of wine.*

Safe carrying

Wicker baskets are good for carrying cutlery, crockery, loaves of bread, crackers, biscuits and cakes. Perishable foods that deteriorate in quality should be carried on chiller packs in insulated bags. Lightweight insulated bags and insulated lunch boxes are practical for out-and-about snacks. Stacking rings that are used to separate plates of food for microwave heating are useful for stacking plated items in a chiller box. Sturdy foods in plastic containers are easier to transport and more successful than delicate items with the potential for ending up as disasters.

Supermarket dash

Simple or special, it is easy to buy a complete picnic menu from a good supermarket or deli without having to compromise on quality. There is more to discover than the usual baguettes, cheese and fruit, so try adding some of the following to the shopping list:
• Breads: select interesting breads, wraps or flour tortillas for scooping up or holding salads, cooked meats or cheese. Try bagels, Italian-style crusty breads or ciabatta, rye breads, naan, mini pitta breads, chapatis, pancakes or crêpes.

Buy a full-flavoured extra virgin olive oil, walnut, macadamia or pumpkin seed oil to go with breads or rolls. Pour a little oil on to saucers and serve chunks of bread to mop it up.
• Salads and vegetables: select washed, ready-to-eat produce that does not have to be cut up but can simply be emptied into bowls and eaten by the sprig without cutlery or as crudités with sour cream, fromage frais, garlic and herb soft cheese, soft goat's cheese or garlic mayonnaise. Among the leaves try watercress, rocket and lamb's lettuce; and select from cherry tomatoes or baby plum tomatoes, trimmed sugar snap peas or mangetouts (snow peas), cauliflower and broccoli florets, baby carrots, baby corn or radishes. Washed parsley, coriander (cilantro) leaves, fennel and basil are also brilliant.

Plain cooked beetroot (beet), vacuum packed without vinegar, is excellent drizzled with walnut oil and sprinkled with ground black pepper; it is also irresistible with soft goat's cheese or mascarpone and a trickle of raspberry vinegar. Canned artichoke hearts are good drained.
• From the deli: smoked salmon or mackerel, pickled herring (packed in oil if possible) and peeled, cooked prawns (shrimp) are versatile with sour cream and lemon wedges. Cured and cooked meats, fish or meat pâtés and terrines are all ideal for picnics. Choose good quality olives and marinated (bell) peppers instead of the mixed salads.

Below *A stylish hamper for carrying china, cutlery and glassware for grand picnic meals.*

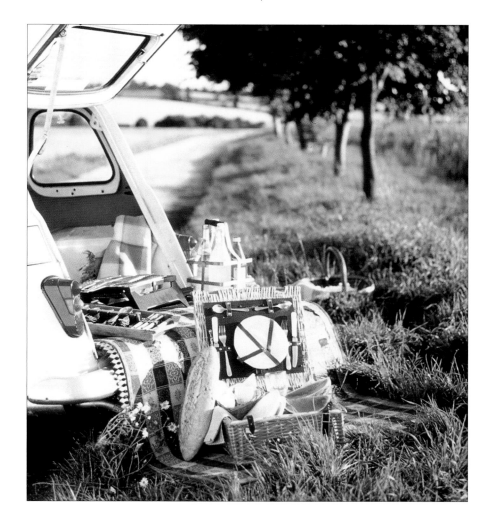

Simply different

These are just a few ideas for dishes that are easy to carry and simple to eat.

• Cut a large loaf into horizontal slices and sandwich them back together with complementary fillings. Wrap tightly in clear film (plastic wrap). Cut into vertical slices to make attractive-looking ribbon sandwiches.

• Slit a large baguette lengthways, scoop out the crumb and fill with layers of mozzarella cheese and roasted spring onions (scallions) and (bell) peppers. Drizzle the layers lightly with good olive oil and sprinkle with shredded basil. Replace the top of the

Below Select alcoholic and non-alcoholic drinks to suit your guests.

baguette, press firmly together and wrap tightly in clear film. Leave overnight in the refrigerator. Cut into wide chunks to serve.

• Sandwich soft wheat tortillas together into a neat stack with a filling of ricotta cheese, salami, cooked chicken and spring onions. Shred the salami and cooked chicken, and chop the spring onions. Spread each tortilla with ricotta and sprinkle with salami, chicken and spring onions before adding the next. Press the stack firmly together and wrap in clear film. Make a spicy tomato salsa to serve with wedges of the tortilla stack.

• Cut short fine strips of spring onion, carrot, cucumber and cooked ham. Thin smooth peanut butter with a little

Above *Filled baguettes in colourful napkins are practical and fun.*

tahini (sesame paste) and olive oil, then add a crushed garlic clove and a few drops of sesame oil. Add a dash of chilli sauce, if you like. Spread this paste thinly over Chinese pancakes and place a little of the shredded vegetables and ham on each. Roll each pancake up tightly and wrap in clear film.

Stepping out

The grand picnic party, so popular with gentility of previous generations, is still a fabulous way of celebrating at a special event. Summer season events such as a day at the races, sailing regattas or country-house operas typify picnic grandeur. The picnic may be served with ceremony and silver at a table (with chauffeur-cum-butler) or for stylish lounging on rugs and large cushions but always with linen napkins, proper cutlery, china and glassware.

• First courses: arrange smoked salmon sandwiches on a serving platter or plates and offer a separate bowl of lemon wedges.

Prepare individual pots of pâté, spread or mousse, sealed with clarified butter and garnished with herb sprigs.

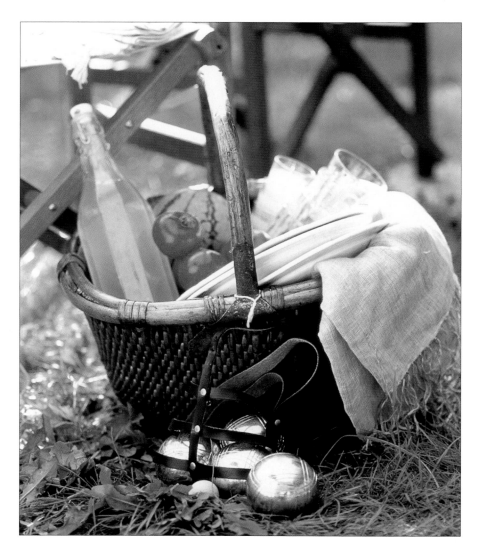

Serve curly Melba toast, rye crisp breads or small shaped dinner rolls as an accompaniment.

Pack chilled soup, such as classic vichyssoise, gazpacho or a fruit soup, in a vacuum flask and take separate containers of cream or chilled garnishing ingredients to add to individual portions.

• The main dish: poached salmon steaks can be dressed at the last minute with a slightly thinned herb or lemon mayonnaise.

An impressive pie or pastry dish, such as game pie or pork pie in large or mini versions, travels well.

Cold roast whole or stuffed boned chicken, turkey, duck or pheasant can be served with a mayonnaise-based sauce or lighter salsa; alternatively, individual boned breast fillets can be coated with mayonnaise and aspic.

Baked glazed ham can be accompanied by pickled peaches poached in spiced syrup made with cider vinegar instead of water.

• Desserts: for exciting fruit salads combine a limited number of complementary fruits, such as

Above *Coleslaw, gherkins and creamy potato salad are all picnic favourites.*

strawberries with papaya and lime, pineapple with mango and toasted shreds of fresh coconut, or physalis with cherries. Whole tropical fruits such as passion fruits, rambutans and mangoes are delicious just on their own.

Fruit tarts and flans filled with confectioner's custard, vanilla custard or a sweetened cream and topped with summer berries are practical when the pastry case is baked in a serving dish.

Set custards baked in individual pots are easy to carry ready for turning out on to serving plates at the last minute.

• And finally, serve two or three perfect cheeses with finger oatcakes, classic Bath Oliver biscuits or plain crackers.

Pack home-made chocolate truffles or high quality after dinner mints in a cool box to serve with coffee. (Take a vacuum flask full of boiling water and instant coffee granules separately rather than keeping the coffee hot for several hours.)

Simple picnic feasts

Try these food combinations for escaping into simple indulgence or to excite the palate as part of an impressive menu:

• Creamy ripe goat's cheese with sweet fresh figs, and take a small pepper mill full of black peppercorns for freshly ground pepper.

• Fine slices of prosciutto, Parma or Serrano ham with little bunches of sweet seedless grapes and lime or lemon wedges.

• Ruffles of finely sliced smoked venison with halved strawberries and cucumber slices.

• Smoked loin of pork and succulent ready-to-eat dried apricots trickled with walnut oil, and lemon wedges.

• Mozzarella cheese slices layered with finely shredded fresh basil and chopped fresh coriander (cilantro) leaves, trickled with good olive oil and served with lemon wedges.

Above *A quick trip to the local deli can provide you with all the picnic basics.*

Outdoor escapes

Summer excursions and picnics may be the main focus for outdoor feasts but there are other occasions when food goes down well in the fresh air:

• On Hallowe'en or bonfire nights cook turkey burgers on the barbecue; wrap potatoes in foil to cook them on the barbecue or pre-bake them in the oven and then finish them on the barbecue. Finish with your favourite muffins, served warm with lots of whipped cream and chocolate sauce.

• The seaside can be exhilarating for winter walks, especially when seafood – large tiger prawns (shrimp) in their shells, prepared squid and skewered swordfish or tuna – is served straight from a portable barbecue and accompanied by pats of garlic and parsley butter with lots of crusty bread. A vacuum flask of light, clear vegetable or seafood broth with chopped herbs and finely diced vegetables goes well with grilled seafood.

• When the snow provides the opportunity for outdoor sport, assemble an impromptu afternoon party with toasted chestnuts, crumpets and English muffins on a barbecue. Mulled wine is a warming drinks option.

party basics

You do not have to be a five-star chef to throw a good party bash but having a few snazzy food and drink ideas to hand is a real help. From exciting deli-selections to confidence with basic recipes, inspiration and essential information are the ingredients for planning the perfect menu.

Just Nibbles

Tune in the party by serving the right type and quantity of snacks with drinks when guests first arrive. Too few or poor quality nibbles look mean and awkward; too many or filling snacks overfill guests before the meal. Flavours should preview the courses to follow; for example, it is not good form to serve powerful, spicy snacks before a delicate meal.

Off-the-shelf selection

The array makes it difficult to resist trying some of the amazing commercial creations, but it is best to do this in your non-entertaining time. Select plain snacks and classic products rather than bizarre concoctions. Many bought savouries are wildly over-seasoned and they completely dull the palate for a delicate meal. Plain salted nuts, Chinese-style rice crackers, simple breadsticks, lightly flavoured croûtons, and good quality crisps (US potato chips) and cocktail crackers complement home-made snacks.

Roasted nuts

Place blanched almonds and plain, shelled pistachio and macadamia nuts in a large, shallow ovenproof dish. Sprinkle with a little salt and cook at 200°C/400°F/Gas 6 for about 6–10 minutes, or until pale golden. Shake the dish well to coat the nuts with the salt and leave to cool. For a deliciously elusive hint of spice, sprinkle the nuts with two or three pinches each of grated nutmeg and ground mace.

Below *Pistachio nuts, almonds and macadamia nuts are good party snacks.*

Above *Good-quality bread, cheese, olives and wine are essential party basics.*

Marinated olives

Lightly crumple 4 bay leaves and place in a small pan with 15ml/1 tbsp fennel seeds, the grated rind of 1 lemon and 2 peeled and sliced garlic cloves. Pour in a little olive oil and cook gently for 15 minutes so that the ingredients barely sizzle. Remove from the heat and whisk in the juice of 1 lemon, 5ml/1 tsp caster (superfine) sugar and a little salt and pepper. Stir in 250ml/8fl oz/1 cup olive oil. Drain a 250g/9oz can pitted black olives in brine, then add them to the oil and mix well. Transfer to a covered container and leave to marinate in the refrigerator for 2–7 days. Drain the olives before serving. (The oil is fabulous for dressing cured meats, vegetables and salads.)

Below *Feta cheese with roast pepper dip with chillies on toast.*

Marinated cheese

Prepare the marinade used for olives to flavour bitesize cubes of feta cheese or mini-mozzarella cheeses. The fennel seeds are good with the cheese but they can be omitted and replaced by several sprigs of fresh oregano instead. Alternatively, instead of fennel and oregano, sprinkle the drained cheese with finely shredded basil when serving. Gouda or Jarlsberg cheese is excellent soaked in the same marinade with fennel, cumin or caraway seeds.

Vegetable crisps

Home-made potato crisps are special when combined with other vegetables, such as beetroot (beet), sweet potatoes, celeriac and carrots.

Peel and thinly slice the potatoes and/or vegetables using a hand peeler, food processor or mandolin. Rinse well in cold water, drain and dry thoroughly on clean dishtowels. Make sure all the slices are separate before deep-frying a handful at a time in hot oil until they

Below *Lemon and herb marinated olives are tasty party nibbles.*

are crisp and golden. Drain thoroughly on paper towels and season lightly with salt.

Roasted cardamom cauliflower florets

Split 8 green cardamom pods and heat gently in a large pan with 60ml/4 tbsp sunflower oil until the pods are just sizzling, then cook for 2 minutes. Break a trimmed cauliflower into bitesize florets. Add the florets to the pan and toss to coat thoroughly in the oil, then turn them out into a shallow ovenproof dish, scraping all the oil over them. Roast at 220°C/425°F/Gas 7 for 10

Above *Spiced plantain chips with hot chilli sauce.*

minutes, turning once, until lightly browned. Season lightly and cool. Discard the cardamoms when transferring the cauliflower florets to serving bowls.

Baguette croûtons

Cut a good baguette with good, soft centre crumb into quarters lengthways. Cut the quarters across into large bitesize chunks. Spread these out in a large roasting pan and bake at 160°C/325°F/Gas 3 for about 40 minutes, turning occasionally, until crisp, dry and lightly browned. Finely chop 1 garlic clove and cook lightly in 30ml/2 tbsp olive oil for 1 minute. Add 5ml/1 tsp each of dried oregano and thyme, then pour in a further 60ml/4 tbsp olive oil. Heat gently for a few minutes, then trickle evenly and thinly over the croûtons. Season lightly with salt and toss well, then return to the oven for a further 5 minutes. Toss with plenty of finely chopped fresh parsley and finely grated lemon rind, if you like, just before serving.

For lightly flavoured croûtons, heat 2 bay leaves, a blade of mace and the pared rind of 1 lemon with the oil instead of the garlic, oregano and thyme. Leave to stand for several hours before pouring over the croûtons.

Salsas, Dips and Dippers

A few good salsas and dips go a long way, and a repertoire of basic recipes can be varied to create exciting snacks. Try them as fillings for hollowed vegetables or halved hard-boiled eggs; spread them on soft tortillas, wraps or pancakes and roll up into tasty picnic snacks or slice them into stylish canapés.

Matching dippers to dips

Vegetable crudités, breadsticks, croûtes and crackers taste good with most dips. For a juicy dip, select dippers to scoop up and hold juice or absorb a little – thick, curly crisps (US potato chips) and tortilla chips work well.

Below *Crunchy tacos are perfect with tomato salsa and guacamole.*

Do's and don'ts for dips and dippers

Do …
• Make smooth, fairly soft, but not sloppy, dips for easy eating.
• Select sturdy and fairly short nibbles to dunk – chunky lengths of celery, carrot, (bell) pepper and fennel; mini breadsticks; pitta bread fingers and crackers.
• Use cocktail sticks (toothpicks) for small, firm bits to dunk.
• Match dippers to dips.
• Serve dips in small bowls on platters, surrounded by enough dippers for the entire bowlful of dip.

Don't …
• Make the dip too thick to scoop easily.
• Prepare dips that separate or become watery on standing.
• Serve fragile dippers that break or bend; avoid fine crisps (US potato chips), fine puff pastries and flopping wedges of pitta.
• Offer nibbles that are too small to dunk without putting your fingers into the dip.
• Serve a huge bowl of dip that does the rounds for 30 minutes only to become messy.
• Offer dressed or sauced dunks that discolour and flavour the dip.

• For crisp potato wedges cut medium to large potatoes into quarters lengthways and place in a plastic bag. Add a little sunflower oil and salt, and then mix well. (Add a generous pinch of dried oregano or rosemary if appropriate for the dip.) Turn out into a roasting pan and cook at 240°C/475°F/Gas 9 for about 40 minutes, turning two or three times, until crisp and browned. Serve freshly cooked.

These can be three-quarters cooked in advance, then finished in the oven at the last minute. Sweet potatoes and new potatoes also work well.
• For crisp skins, halve baked potatoes and scoop out the middle, leaving a fairly thick shell. Brush all over with oil, place in a greased roasting pan and season lightly with salt. Roast at 200°C/400°F/Gas 6 for about 30 minutes, or until crisp and browned.

Red salsa

Play with this basic mixture to impress your personality on it and excite your palate – add a little extra sugar or chilli, perhaps, and increase the paprika for a deeper, warmer flavour. To lighten the salsa and add a lively zing, omit the tomato purée (paste) and stir in a little lemon juice. The salsa complements fish, poultry, meat or cheese; it makes a terrific dip with fingers of pitta bread or cheese cubes on sticks; and it is delicious on bitesize croûtes, topped with halved, hard-boiled quails' eggs.

Mix 60ml/4 tbsp tomato purée, 1 finely chopped red onion, 1 seeded and finely chopped red (bell) pepper, 1 seeded and finely chopped mild red chilli, 1 crushed garlic clove, 10ml/2 tsp caster (superfine) sugar, 2.5ml/½ tsp paprika and 30ml/2 tbsp balsamic vinegar until thoroughly combined. Peel and chop 450g/1lb ripe tomatoes, then stir them into the mixture. Add salt and pepper to taste. Cover and chill for 1–3 days in the refrigerator.

Cucumber and avocado salsa

This fresh, lively salsa complements fish and seafood, salami and cured meats, and grilled (broiled) and barbecued meats and burgers. It enlivens creamy cheeses. As a dip, it is wicked with potato wedges or skins, and chunky cheese straws.

Peel and finely chop 1 cucumber, then place it in a sieve. Sprinkle with

Below *Tomato-based salsas are very versatile: add chillies, coriander or garlic.*

salt and leave over a bowl to drain for 30 minutes. Meanwhile, finely chop 1 large seeded green (bell) pepper, 1 seeded mild green chilli, 1 bunch of spring onions (scallions) and mix with 15ml/1 tbsp caster sugar, 45ml/3 tbsp good olive oil and the grated rind and juice of 1 lime. Squeeze the cucumber and then dry it on kitchen paper before adding it to the salsa. Halve, stone (pit) and finely chop 2 avocados, then mix them into the salsa. Chop a big bunch of coriander (cilantro) leaves and stir them into the salsa.

Cover and chill for several hours or up to 1 day. Before serving, finely shred a handful of tender basil sprigs and stir them in.

Below *Pitta bread makes excellent dippers for creamy dips.*

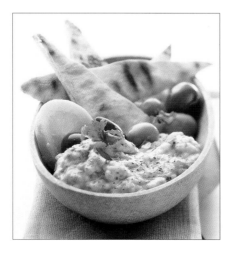

Above *Spicy pumpkin dip served with cucumber crudités.*

Onion and chive dip

This is delicious as a filling for baked potatoes or with crispy barbecue-cooked new potatoes; it is a good accompaniment for baked gammon or a filling for cherry tomatoes.

Peel and quarter 6 onions. Mix 15ml/1 tbsp sugar, 15ml/1 tbsp wholegrain mustard, 30ml/2 tbsp sunflower oil and 30ml/2 tbsp cider vinegar in a shallow ovenproof dish just large enough to hold the onions. Turn the onions in this mixture, then roast at 200°C/400°F/Gas 6 for about 45 minutes, turning once or twice, until tender. Cover and cool.

Purée the onions with their juices. Gradually stir the onion purée into 450g/1lb curd cheese. Finely snip a handful of chives into the dip, add a little freshly grated nutmeg and mix well. Taste for seasoning, then chill.

Gorgonzola and parsley dip

Mash 225g/8oz Gorgonzola cheese and mix in 225g/8oz/1 cup ricotta cheese. Finely chop 50g/2oz flat leaf parsley and mix it into the dip with freshly ground black pepper. Stir in 250ml/8fl oz/1 cup crème fraîche and seasoning to taste. Chill before serving.

Salad Talk

In a flurry of curly leaves or a frisée of fine shreds, every salad should make a stunning statement. Move on from making irrelevant "side salads" to presenting classy creations by marrying vegetables with taste bud-tingling dressings and well-textured toppings.

Salad reminders

Harmonize all aspects of a salad; the base, main ingredients, dressing and topping or garnish should contrast and blend to perfection.

• Include a limited selection of complementary flavours and textures rather than a mishmash of ingredients – this is especially relevant with rice or pasta salads.

• Dress leafy salads at the last minute, otherwise they become limp. For buffets, serve the dressing separately.

• Sprinkle crisp or crunchy toppings over when serving, or offer them separately for buffets.

• Have a generous taste of the dressing to check the seasoning and balance of

Below *Classic Caesar salad is a popular party dish.*

Above *Olive oil and ripe black olives add plenty of flavour.*

sweet to sour. The dressing must complement not mask the salad.

• There should be enough dressing to coat but not drown the ingredients.

• Light-textured and thin dressings complement soft and crisp ingredients; crunchy and firm ingredients support creamy coatings.

• Unless they should be served chilled, remove salads from the refrigerator about 30 minutes before serving.

Full-of-flavour leaves

The palate-cleansing properties of fresh leaves are welcome with firm, substantial main dishes, such as grilled poultry or meat and hearty raised pies or pastries. They are also an excellent base for sautéed or grilled fish and seafood, finely sliced cured meats or crumbly or creamy cheeses.

For exciting leafy ensembles mix green flavours with subtly different textures. Crisp iceberg, cos or romaine lettuces contrast with lamb's lettuce, lollo rosso or Little Gem (Bibb) leaves.

Baby spinach brings a firm, rather than crisp, texture and a subtle, slightly musty flavour. Peppery watercress and savoury rocket (arugula) bring positive textures as well as lively flavour.

Herb sprigs are excellent in leafy salads, either singly or in a burst of mixed flavours. Chopping the herbs changes the result completely, distributing their flavour rather than providing the occasional interesting mouthful; so include small sprig ends with their tender edible stems.

Salad portions

Estimating salad portions for large gatherings is not easy; simply multiplying portion sizes for a meal for four or six by a larger number for a buffet does not work. Portion sizes are smaller for buffet salads. As a rough guide for gatherings of over 20, 1 large lettuce (lollo rosso, iceberg, cos or romaine) will provide eight portions, 500g/1¼lb tomatoes will be enough for six, 1 small white cabbage will serve 12 when finely shredded, 500g/1¼lb new potatoes will serve four and 500g/1¼lb shredded carrots will serve six to eight.

The crunch factor

The greater resistance of crunch is different from crisp and it is a texture that supports substantial ingredients and flavours or creamy dressings very well. Fennel, celery, radishes, cucumber, carrots, celeriac, red or white cabbage, courgettes (zucchini), (bell) peppers, beansprouts and onions are packed with crunch. For super-crunchy salads, add drained and thinly sliced canned water chestnuts.

Tender not soft

Cooked root vegetables, tomatoes, mushrooms, canned bamboo shoots and olives are examples of tender ingredients that can be marinated in dressings to impart or absorb flavours. A suitable marinade should not spoil their textures but it will enrich the salad and give it depth.

Tip-top finishes

The decorative garnishes or toppings for salad add vital flavour and introduce interesting textures.

• Chopped, slivered or whole nuts can complement main ingredients or be a focal point. Walnuts, pecans, pistachios, macadamia nuts and hazelnuts are all excellent on salads.

• Lightly roasted seeds bring strength of flavour and texture. Linseeds, pumpkin, sesame, sunflower, mustard and poppy seeds are all delicious individually or together. Pine nuts are delicious, tender and nutty and go especially well with spinach.

• Lightly roasted grains bring texture and flavour, and they go well with seeds and/or bacon. Barley, rye and/or oat flakes can all be roasted in a dry, heavy pan until lightly browned and crisp.

• Croûtons bring crunch and they can be tasty with herbs and/or garlic.

• Crisp sautéed diced bacon or gammon, salami or chorizo are full of flavour and texture.

Above *White beans with green peppers in a spicy dressing.*

Asides to centrepieces

Salads make appealing first courses or light main courses and many are just a twist away from becoming impressive centrepieces for picnics or buffets. The trick is to marry punchy main ingredients with a salad base full of character, then link them with a sympathetic dressing. Experiment with the following examples:

• A substantial full-flavoured leaf and herb base is brilliant for pan-fried fish, poultry, cheese or tofu. Sliced scallops, peeled raw tiger prawns (shrimp), chunks of salmon, strips of chicken or turkey breast fillet, cubes of halloumi cheese or firm tofu can all be

marinated with a little olive oil, garlic and lemon rind, then pan-fried and tossed into the salad while hot. Deglaze the pan with lemon juice or balsamic vinegar, a sprinkling of sugar, seasoning and a final drizzle of olive oil to make a delicious dressing. To serve the salad cold, transfer the pan-fried ingredients to a container, pour over the deglazed dressing and cool, then mix with the leaves before serving.

• Use shredded crunchy salad in a light oil-based dressing as a base for ruffles of thinly sliced cured meats; julienne of cooked meats; quartered hard-boiled eggs and diced smoked salmon or ham; or diced firm cheese. Add a creamy dressing and crunchy topping.

• A mixture of soft and crisp, lightly flavoured leaves (for example lollo biondo, lamb's lettuce and shredded iceberg) is a good base for fresh fruit, rich dried fruit and creamy cheese. Crisp and juicy green grapes, sliced dried apricots and sliced ripe Brie combine well. Add a topping of coarsely chopped walnuts and dress with a drizzle of walnut oil. Add lemon wedges as a little zest to taste.

Below *Refreshing tabbouleh with masses of chopped fresh herbs.*

Sauces, Dressings and Relishes

A good home-made sauce elevates plain cooked foods to a stylish dish. Here are a few classic recipes:

Tomato sauce

This good basic sauce freezes well. Thaw it for several hours at room temperature or in the microwave. Apart from the myriad of uses in compound dishes, the sauce goes well with plain cooked fish, poultry or meat.

For the simplest informal supper party, serve fresh pasta with tomato sauce, topped with lots of finely shredded fresh basil and coriander (cilantro), and shavings of Parmesan cheese. Add a punchy, crunchy salad of shredded fennel and white cabbage with chopped spring onion (scallion) and toasted pine nuts.

Chop 1 onion, 1 celery stick, 1 carrot and 1 garlic clove, then cook in 30ml/2 tbsp olive oil with 2 bay leaves and 1 large sprig each of fresh thyme and oregano for 15 minutes. Cover the pan to keep the moisture in and prevent the vegetables from browning. Add 1kg/2lb chopped ripe tomatoes, 30ml/2 tbsp tomato purée

(paste), 15ml/1 tbsp sugar, 2.5ml/½ tsp paprika and a little seasoning. Heat, stirring, until the tomatoes give up some of their juice, and simmer then cover the pan and cook gently for 40–45 minutes, until the vegetables are tender and the tomatoes reduced. Discard the bay leaves and herb sprigs, then purée the sauce. Use the sauce as it is (slightly coarse) or press it through a fine sieve for a smooth texture.

Mayonnaise

Home-made mayonnaise is superb, and the flavour can be fine-tuned to your personal taste by adjusting the balance of sunflower and olive oils (or using different types of oil) and the quantity of lemon juice.

Home-made mayonnaise contains raw egg; pregnant women, the very young and the elderly are generally advised not to eat raw eggs.

Commercial mayonnaise, however, is pasteurized to destroy any micro-organisms in the egg and it can be a safer option for buffet dishes that are likely to be left sitting for several hours in a warm room.

Below *Pickles add full flavour to accompaniments and condiments.*

Below *Home-made garlic mayonnaise with crudités.*

Above *Home-made mayonnaise is quick to make and so delicious.*

Use an electric beater to whisk 1 large (US extra large) egg with a little salt and pepper, 2.5ml/½ tsp Dijon mustard and the juice of ½ small lemon, until thoroughly combined. Mix 150ml/¼ pint/⅔ cup each of sunflower and olive oil. Whisking constantly, gradually add the oils to the egg in a very thin trickle, broken at first, then more constantly as the mixture thickens and becomes creamy. The finished mayonnaise should be thick, pale and glossy. Add salt, pepper and lemon juice to taste if required.

• The mayonnaise can be made in a food processor by processing the egg mixture first, then gradually dropping and trickling in the oil with the motor running. Scrape the mixture down frequently. A large food processor bowl may be too large for a single quantity.

• For a rich mayonnaise, use egg yolks rather than whole egg and allow 2 egg yolks to 250 ml/8 fl oz/1 cup oil.

Flavouring mayonnaise

A well-flavoured mayonnaise can be served as a filling for baked potatoes or a dip with potato wedges.

• Add 1 crushed garlic clove to the egg. For a mellow flavour, first cook 1 garlic clove in a little olive oil until lightly browned.

• Stir in 60ml/4 tbsp chopped fresh chives, parsley, tarragon, dill or fennel, or a handful of shredded basil leaves.

• Stir in the grated rind of 1 lemon, lime or orange. Use the juice of 1 lime instead of the lemon juice. (Orange juice is not sharp enough to balance the oil and egg mixture.)

• To make a spicy rouille, add 1 crushed garlic clove, 5ml/1 tsp paprika and a good pinch of cayenne pepper to the egg. Taste the prepared mayonnaise for seasoning and add a little extra cayenne if you like. Rouille is a traditional accompaniment for fish soups, served with slices of warm baguette, but it also goes with a wide variety of other foods or it makes a delicious dip for plain breadsticks.

Excellent salad dressing

This is a good basic oil and vinegar salad dressing, which can be varied to suit all sorts of salads. Different types of oil (sunflower, grapeseed, walnut, hazelnut or pumpkin seed) or vinegar (remember all the flavoured vinegars) can be used, and there are many types of mustard that will vary the flavour. Strong nut oils should be used in modest amounts with light grapeseed or sunflower oil.

Below Good quality olive oil adds a unique flavour.

Above Quail's eggs served with mayonnaise dip and olive oil.

Whisk 5ml/1 tsp sugar, salt and freshly ground black pepper, and 7.5ml/1½ tsp mustard (wholegrain or Dijon, mild or strong to taste) with 30ml/2 tbsp balsamic or cider vinegar until the sugar and salt have dissolved. Whisking hard and constantly, slowly pour in 150ml/¼ pint/⅔ cup olive oil. The dressing will emulsify and thicken slightly. Store in an airtight jar in the refrigerator and shake before serving.

Flavouring dressings

Try some of the following additions.

• Add 1 chopped garlic clove.

• Add 30ml/2 tbsp chopped parsley, mint, tarragon or chives.

• Add the grated rind of ½–1 lemon.

• To make a spicy peanut dressing, omit the mustard and use 30ml/2 tbsp crunchy peanut butter. Add the juice of 1 lime and a pinch of dried red chillies.

Beetroot relish

This sweet and sour preserve is terrific with hot or cold meats or with cheese. Serve it with a Christmas buffet or a summer barbecue.

Peel and coarsely grate 450g/1lb raw beetroot (beet). Peel, core and coarsely grate 450g/1lb cooking apples.

Finely chop 450g/1lb onions. Peel and chop 25g/1oz fresh root ginger. Mix all the ingredients in a pan and add 2 crushed garlic cloves, 5ml/1 tsp each of ground cinnamon and nutmeg, 225g/8oz/1 cup soft brown sugar and 450ml/¾ pint/scant 2 cups cider vinegar. Bring to the boil, stirring occasionally, then reduce the heat and cover the pan. Simmer the relish for about 1½ hours. Pot the relish in warmed sterilized jars immediately the pan is removed from the heat. Cover with airtight lids and store for at least 2 weeks before eating. It makes about 1.3kg/3lb.

Below Beetroot relish.

Making the Best of Bread

The advantage of baking your own bread is that you can create individual rolls or loaves to complement the menu or to become a real feature on their own, especially for breakfast, brunch, lunch or late suppers. Breads can be baked or bought well in advance and frozen. Seek out interesting breads and discover lots of ways of using them.

• Wholemeal bread: use wholemeal (whole-wheat) flour and add an extra 50ml/2fl oz/¼ cup water.

• Seeded breads: use all wholemeal or half and half wholemeal and white. Add 15ml/1 tbsp each of caraway and cumin seeds, and 30ml/2 tbsp each of poppy and sesame seeds.

• Rye bread: use half rye flour and half white flour. Add 30ml/2 tbsp caraway seeds and an extra 50ml/2fl oz/¼ cup water to the mixture.

Below *For a party, buy interesting bread flavoured with seeds and herbs.*

• Milk bread: use hand-hot milk instead of water for richer bread. Rub 50g/2oz/¼ cup butter into the flour before adding the yeast, salt and sugar then omit the olive oil. Do not glaze the bread before baking.

• Herb bread: add 10ml/2 tsp dried sage, 10ml/2 tsp dried thyme and 60ml/4 tbsp chopped fresh chives to the flour. Also try oregano, dill, fennel, coriander (cilantro) and parsley.

Shaping dough

Make interestingly shaped loaves for a special occasion.

• Braid: cut the dough into thirds and roll these into long, thin strips. Pinch the ends of the strips together, and then braid them. Leave to rise, brush with beaten egg and sprinkle with poppy seeds before baking. Use milk bread for a richer dough.

• Oval loaves: cut the dough in half and shape each piece into a roll about

Basic bread dough

Mix 450g/1lb strong plain white bread flour with 1 sachet fast action easy-blend (rapid-rise) dried yeast, 5ml/1 tsp salt and 5ml/1 tsp sugar. Make a well in the middle and add 250ml/8fl oz/1 cup hand-hot water and 30ml/2 tbsp olive oil. Gradually work the liquid into the flour to make a stiff dough. Turn the dough out on to a lightly floured surface and knead it for about 10 minutes, or until very smooth and elastic. Shape the dough as required and place on a greased baking tray. Cover with oiled clear film (plastic wrap) and leave in a warm place until doubled in size before baking. Bake large loaves at 220°C/425°F/Gas 7 for about 40 minutes, or until well risen and browned. Bake rolls at the same temperature for 20–25 minutes. Turn the bread over and tap the base: the loaf should sound hollow. If it sounds damp and solid it is not properly cooked through so return it to the oven for a further 5 minutes and check again.

20cm/8in long. Leave to rise, then use a sharp knife to cut shallow diagonal slits across the top before brushing with a little warm water and baking.

• Rolls: cut the dough into 12 equal portions and shape these into round or oval rolls. To make a knot, roll a portion into a thin strip and twist it into a knot. For twists, divide each portion in half, roll into strips and twist these together. Transfer the rolls to a greased baking tray and leave to rise. Brush with beaten egg or milk, then sprinkle with sesame or poppy seeds before baking.

• Swirl: make up two batches of dough: one plain white and one

Above *Warm, fresh home-baked bread can be a real feature at parties.*

seeded half and half wholemeal and white. Cut each type in half. Roll out a portion of white into an oval, and then roll a portion of seeded into a equal-size oval. Lay the seeded dough on the white and roll up both into an oval loaf. Repeat with the remaining dough to make a second loaf. Leave to rise, brush with warm water and sprinkle with seeds before baking.

Buying guide

Buy bread on the day it is to be eaten or buy and freeze it in advance, then thaw it early on the day or overnight.
• Crusty breads, such as baguettes, French and Italian country breads, and the British bloomer, are good for mopping up dressings and sauces, and they go well with cheese. Cut them into chunks to make crusty croûtons.
• Rich breads, such as milk bread, brioche or challah/cholla, are a good choice for brunch or to accompany marinated vegetables and salads for lunch. They are excellent for picnics.
• Flat breads, such as pitta, naan or soft wheat tortillas, can be used more widely than in their traditional roles. They go well with dips or pâtés, and are good filled or topped with salads, roasted vegetables, grilled or cured meat.

• Individual breads are perfect for buffets, picnics, breakfast or brunch. Croissants, bagels, English muffins and crumpets, teacakes or currant buns are real treat breads, as good packed with fabulous fillings as they are served in traditional style.
• Close-textured or coarse breads bring out the best in smoked fish, seafood, cured meats, fine pâtés and cheese. While firm dark or light rye bread can be thinly sliced, the coarser grainy breads tend to be more crumbly and are good served in thick chunks.

Serving bread

Warm bread has a better flavour and texture than cold.
• Present a whole loaf on a cutting board, with knife. For a large party, when guests are less likely to slice their own bread, the loaf may be part or completely sliced and presented with the slices re-assembled to prevent them from drying out.
• Pile warm flat or individual breads in a linen-lined basket and fold the cloth over to keep the bread warm.
• Sliced baguette and thinly cut breads complement light first courses; chunks, wedges and hearty lengths of baguette are more filling with main dishes and substantial salads.

Hot savoury breads

Slice a baguette, bloomer or crusty French country bread ring, leaving the slices attached at the base. Spread one of the following fillings on the slices and press them back together. Spread a little extra filling over the top. Wrap the loaf in foil and heat in the oven at 200°C/400°F/Gas 6 for about 15 minutes. Serve hot.
• Garlic butter: cream 115g/4oz/½ cup butter with 1 crushed garlic clove.
• Herb butter: cream 60ml/4 tbsp chopped fresh herbs into 115g/4oz/ ½ cup butter.

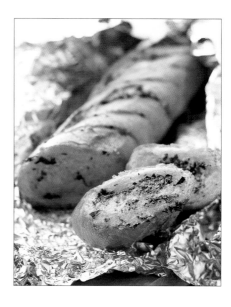

Above *Serve garlic or herby buttered baguettes warm and with napkins.*

• Anchovy and olive butter: finely chop a 50g/2oz can anchovies in olive oil, and cream with 115g/4oz/½ cup butter, gradually working in the oil from the can. Add 115g/4oz chopped black olives, a squeeze of lemon juice and freshly ground black pepper.
• Spring onion, lime and coriander butter: finely chop 4 spring onions (scallions) and a good handful of fresh coriander leaves, then cream with 115g/4oz/½ cup butter, adding the grated rind of 1 lime and a squeeze of lime juice. Add a chopped garlic clove, if you like.

Croûtons and croûtes

These can be cut into small cubes or chunks to match any dishes. Sauté them in olive oil and butter or bake until crisp and lightly browned, then drizzle with a little oil. Alternatively, lightly brush slices of bread with oil and grill (broil) until golden, then cut into cubes.
• Croûtes are bread slices, brushed with melted butter or oil, and baked, grilled or fried until golden on both sides. They may be small and thin, or thick and crusty slices. Croûtes complement soft foods or make a good base to absorb juices.

Stunning Cheese Boards

Whether the cheese board is an international extravaganza or a celebration of one or two good cheeses depends on the occasion and the role of the cheese in the menu.

Dinner-party cheese course

When the cheese board is served as a dinner-party course among many there may be just one or two cheeses or a small selection of different types. Offering one fine example is quite acceptable, typically Brie or a similar universally popular type of cheese. It is fun to focus on something special you know your guests will appreciate, such as a good blue or tangy goat's cheese.

The more usual approach to the basic dinner-party cheese board is to include an example each of hard, blue and semi-soft cheese. One or two other cheeses are often added according to what is good at the deli. Availability and quality are important and it is better to limit the cheeses to a few good quality examples than to offer many second-rate selections.

Above *Keep to a few fresh, good-quality cheeses for the cheese board.*

• Vary the sizes, shapes and textures of pieces of cheese.
• Ensure that there is enough of each cheese for every guest to have a modest sample; buy more than one of a small cheese if necessary.
• Cheese may be served after the main course and before dessert, in the French style, or after the dessert and before coffee. If it is practical, the cheese can be brought to the table and offered at the same time as the dessert, allowing individuals to decide which they would prefer to eat first.

Cheese on the buffet

The selection of cheeses may be one of many courses of food or it may be the main focus for a buffet. The modern cheese and wine party is way beyond squares of hard cheese on sticks: it is a celebration of cheese.
• When serving a wide variety, keep the different types of cheese separate. Large pieces can be given their own

platters or stands. If there is more than one type of hard white, semi-soft or blue cheese, group them by type on separate boards or platters.
• Contrasting colours and shapes are important, so include cheeses with different rinds, and display logs, pyramids, squares, domes or rounds as well as wedges and wheels.
• One or more whole cheeses in perfect condition are a real delight. Order from a good supplier well in advance, requesting that the cheese be in peak condition for the party. A whole Brie and a half or whole Stilton are a good classic combination.

Presentation tips

Wooden or marble boards are traditional but china platters and glass or china cake stands work extremely well. Baskets lined with heavy linen napkins, topped with fresh vine leaves are an attractive backdrop for cheese.
• Remove cheese from the refrigerator several hours beforehand and leave it in a cool room. Unwrap any pre-packed cheeses and cover them loosely.
• Always have separate knives for hard, soft, blue and goat's cheeses.
• Allow enough space on the board or base for cutting.
• Do not clutter a board with grapes if it already contains several cheeses; it is better to serve the fruit separately.

Below *Remove cheese from the refrigerator shortly before serving.*

Accompaniments

Crackers should be plain. Oatcakes, water biscuits, Bath Oliver biscuits and Melba toast are excellent. Flavoured and salted biscuits ruin good cheese.

• Crusty bread with plenty of substantial, soft crumb should be offered as well as biscuits. When offering cheese as the main food for a meal or buffet, choose a good selection of breads that are light in flavour but substantial in texture.

• Serve bowls of watercress or rocket (arugula) sprigs with the cheese. A light green salad can clear the palate.

• Celery sticks and pieces of fennel.

• Fresh figs, apples, pears, grapes, physalis, fresh dates and apricots go well with all cheeses. Dried fruits to serve with cheese include apricots, dates, peaches, pears and figs.

• Nuts in the shell or shelled.

• When serving cheese as a main course, black or green olives, or sweet ripe tomatoes may be offered.

• Chutneys, pickles, relishes and salsas are delicious with a main-course cheese board. Sweet-sour flavours are particularly successful.

Below *Chopped egg and onions with white cheese and olives.*

Above *Edible flowers, such as scented geraniums, add flavour and interest.*

• Offer an excellent oil with the cheese – walnut, hazelnut, macadamia or olive oils may be trickled on a plate as a condiment for cheese.

Lower-fat options

Watching everyone else indulge in a lavish cheese course is dismal for guests who have to limit their intake of saturated fat. It is possible to offer lower-fat options without compromising on quality.

• Ricotta cheese is available in low-fat versions and is delicious with fresh or dried fruit. Slit and stone (pit) fresh dates, separate the halves leaving them joined underneath, fill with ricotta and top with a fine shaving of Parmesan.

• Creamy medium-fat soft goat's cheese is delicious with fresh figs. Slit each fig almost down into quarters, leaving them joined at the base. Fill with soft goat's cheese and serve with freshly ground black pepper.

• Sandwich walnut halves together with low-fat soft cheese.

• Slit ready-to-eat dried apricots and fill them with a little low-fat soft cheese, then add a young mint leaf to each.

• Ready-to-eat dried apricots are delicious with feta cheese. Place small cubes of feta in slit apricots.

• Make delicious potted cheese with nuts by mixing very finely chopped walnuts with low-fat soft cheese. Add a little walnut oil to intensify the flavour, if you like. Pistachio nuts and pistachio nut oil can also be used – do not chop the nuts as finely as the walnuts and use the pistachio nut oil sparingly as it is very strong. Serve with celery and fennel.

Cheese savouries

Hot savouries can be served instead of a cheese board. The important point is to keep everything small to add a final burst of flavour at the end of the meal or before the dessert rather than to introduce another filling course.

A small pot of cheese fondue, neat fingers of cheese on toast or Welsh rarebit are all suitable. Little croûtes topped with goat's cheese and grilled (broiled) can be served with peppery watercress or rocket. Miniature tartlets made with cheese pastry can be filled with warm Stilton topped with a grape.

Below *A small pot of cheese fondue can be served as the final course.*

Wine for All Occasions

The variety of drinks available, as well as attitudes to entertaining and drinking have changed significantly in the last couple of decades such that providing liquid refreshment involves more than buying a few anonymous bottles of red and white wine. There is better information in supermarkets, and wine merchants who provide reliable, practical advice are no longer limited to élite outlets. Parties offering an "open bar" are not common but it is usual to offer a mixed selection of pre-dinner drinks. Cocktail parties are fun occasions and can be combined with dressing up in 1920s style.

Whatever the occasion or refreshment, non-alcoholic drinks are important, as most people prefer to avoid alcohol completely when they are driving and many also prefer to drink small amounts. Generous quantities of table water are essential at every meal to complement wine, and a selection of sophisticated alcohol-free aperitifs should be offered on every occasion.

Below *Choose a selection of red and white wines to suit different tastes.*

Above *There is a choice of several wine glasses from your wine merchant.*

Party wines

For the majority of parties it is still usual to provide white or red wine. Offering a choice of dry to medium-dry white is a good idea, especially when the menu is finger food rather than a main meal. Medium-bodied and soft reds are more flexible than their robust counterparts. Take advantage of wine-tasting opportunities at supermarkets, wine merchants or warehouses, particularly the latter where there is always a selection of wines for tasting.

Sparkling white wine is fun for parties, but always offer still wine as an alternative. Champagne is the choice for special celebrations. If you are planning a large gathering and want to serve expensive wines, it is worth taking expert and practical advice from a reputable wine merchant. You may well find expensive wines and sparkling wines offered there on a sale-or-return basis for whole cases.

Wine with food

The tradition of serving white wine with fish or poultry, and red with meat or cheese is still a good rule of thumb, but the vastly increased choice and changing cooking styles have widened the goalposts dramatically. Personal wine preference is just as important as bowing to expert opinion, so if you want to share your favourite wines with friends, do not feel inhibited even if they do not feature in wine guides or fashionable columns.

As a general rule, match light foods with light wines; crisp textures with crisp wines; and robust foods with characterful or full-bodied wines. Never

Below Sparkling wine or champagne is popular for a special occasion.

Above *Crisp, dry white wines complement seafood and poultry.*

make the mistake of using cheap and nasty wine in special cooking but use a good wine and complement it by serving the same or similar at the table. For example, when cooking fish, poultry or meat in wine or serving a wine sauce buy enough wine for cooking and serving with the meal.

First courses

When champagne or sparkling wine is offered as an aperitif it is often served for the first course. Light and crisp white wines complement salad-style appetizers and fine soups, while slightly more complex or fuller whites support fish or vegetables, pâté and egg dishes.

Fish, poultry and meat

• Fish and shellfish take crisp, dry white wines, including Sauvignon Blanc, Chablis, Muscadet sur lie or Chardonnay from Alto Adige. Firm-fleshed fish, shellfish and richer fish dishes or pâtés take the more robust whites, such as white Rioja, Australian Sémillon, oaked Chardonnays, and Californian Fumé Blanc.
• Chicken takes a soft red, such as mature burgundy, Crianza, Reserva Rioja or Californian Merlot. Light cooking methods, such as poaching in white wine, call for lighter wine but

Above *Choose full-bodied reds to accompany beef or pork.*

this could well be a rich white to match a creamy sauce.
• Turkey is slightly more powerful than chicken. An impressive red is essential for Thanksgiving or Christmas. St-Emilion, Pomerol claret, Châteauneuf-du-Pape, Australian Cabernet-Merlot or Cabernet Shiraz blends are all suitable.
• Duck benefits from a young red with some acidity, such as Crozes-Hermitage, Chianti Classico or Californian or New Zealand Pinot.
• Game birds take a fully aged Pinot Noir from the Côte d'Or, Carneros or Oregon while powerful venison is matched by concentrated red Bordeaux or northern Rhône wines, or Cabernet Shiraz and Zinfandel.
• Beef takes medium- to full-bodied reds. Serve reds from lighter Bordeaux wines or a medium Châteauneuf-du-Pape to the most powerful Zinfandels, Barolo, Barbaresco or Coonawarra Shiraz. Syrah or Grenache match mustard and horseradish condiments.
• Cabernet Sauvignon complements lamb, especially ripe examples from any of the producing countries.
• Pork takes full-bodied, slightly spicy reds, such as southern Rhône blends, Australian Shiraz, California Syrah or Tuscan Vino Nobile or Brunello.

Pasta

Match the wine to the sauce or type of pasta dish, for example the dominant flavours may be fish, poultry or meat. Light to medium reds go well with tomato-based sauces. Good Soave complements creamy pasta dishes, especially those containing seafood.

Desserts

Sauternes, Barsac and Monbazillac are classic wines for creamy desserts and custards. Rich Sauternes and high-alcohol dessert wines complement chocolate desserts. German or Austrian Rieslings or late-harvest Muscat from North America are great with baked fruit desserts and tarts. Slightly sweeter sparkling wines, such as Asti or Moscato d'Asti, are light and wash down Christmas pudding, gâteaux and meringues. Rich desserts, fruit cakes and nut-based specialities, such as pecan pie, will take a liqueur Muscat, sweet oloroso sherry or Madeira.

Cheese

Traditionally, cheese was always served with red wine, and although the combination of full rich and powerful

Below High-alcohol dessert wines go especially well with chocolate desserts.

cheese with a full red is an enjoyable one, the very heavy, tannic wines tend to mask the subtle nuttiness and lingering slight sweetness that comes with good ripe cheese.

Happily, the picture is now a little more varied. Any red wine or substantial white served with the main course can be finished off with cheese. Selecting wine to complement cheese is different and the idea of matching flavours and full-ness is a good one to consider. Fresh, crisp and slightly acidic and dry cheeses are best matched by crisp, fruity wines. Mellow, richer and creamy cheese takes a more rounded white, such as a full Chardonnay, or a light red. Blue cheeses are well matched by sweet wines.

- As a general rule, offer a choice of a substantial white and a soft red.
- Light whites, such as Sauvignon or Chenin Blanc, go well with light

Above Whatever type you select, always go for a good quality corkscrew.

cheeses, such as the crumbly mild whites and fresh light goat's cheese.
- Chianti, Merlot or Rioja support the more substantial, ripe and well-flavoured semi-soft cheeses.
- New Zealand Cabernet Sauvignon or Côte du Rhône marry well with the medium-strong hard cheeses.
- Save Australian Shiraz and Californian Cabernet Sauvignon for well-matured hard cheese.
- Fruity wines, such as Vouvray, Chenin Blanc or rosé, match mild and creamy blue cheese while the stronger blues with a piquant flavour take the more robust reds.
- Sweet wines, such as Monbazillac, complement the stronger blue cheeses. Classic combinations include port with Stilton and Sauternes with Roquefort.

Serving wine

Much of the ceremony and paraphernalia of wine opening is conspicuous rather than practical.

Temperature

White wines should be chilled and reds served at room temperature. Over-chilling whites dulls their flavour – light whites should be served at 10°C/50°F, or just below, while the fuller Chardonnays, dry Sémillons and Alsace wines can be slightly less cool. The chilling time depends on the starting temperature of the bottle, but as a general rule allow a couple of hours in the refrigerator.

Leave red wines in a warm room for a couple of hours before serving. Heating them on a radiator is a bad idea as this clouds the flavours and aromas. Some light reds, such as young Beaujolais, can be served lightly chilled.

Allowing wine to breathe

Opening red wine in advance and allowing it to breathe before drinking is intended to take the tannic or acidic edge off the flavour of young reds. However, as the amount of air that

Below *Sniff lightly and long, with the nose slightly below the rim of the glass.*

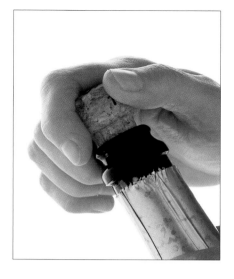

Above *When opening sparkling wines, control the release of the cork.*

gets at the wine through the top of the bottle is minimal, unless the wine is decanted into a jug (pitcher) or carafe, merely opening the bottle normally has very little effect.

Decanting

This involves pouring wine off the sediment that has formed in the bottle. Leave the bottle to stand upright undisturbed overnight so that all the sediment sinks to the bottom. Open the bottle gently and pour the wine into the decanter in a slow steady

Below *A foil cutter removes a neat circle from the seal over the cork.*

Above *This type of corkscrew requires the minimum of effort.*

stream, keeping the bottle at a minimum angle the whole time to retain the sediment in the bottom. Keep your eye on the sediment and stop pouring as soon as it reaches the neck of the bottle. If there is more than half a glass of wine left, strain it through muslin.

Opening

Sparkling wine or chilled champagne will not go off like a cannon if properly opened, providing it has not been vigorously moved or shaken.

Have the glasses ready. Remove the foil and wire, holding the cork firmly in place. Hold the cork with one hand and the bottom part of the bottle with the other. Keep a firm hold on the cork. Concentrate on twisting the bottle, not the cork, until you feel the cork beginning to yield. Once it begins to go, the cork will push itself out, so the aim is to control its exit rather than leaving go and letting it pop out. The cork often needs a slight twist to help it on its way – just help it to move gently in the opposite direction to the bottle.

Pour a third to half a glass first to prevent the sparkling wine or champagne from overflowing, then go round again topping up the glasses when the first foam has subsided.

Organizing Drinks, Glasses and Quantities

If you intend making an open offer of drinks, make sure guests know what is available. Tell them or display the bottles on a table or set up a bar.

As a rule, include gin, vodka, whisky, sherry and dry white vermouth as a basic selection. Rum, Campari, red vermouth and sweet white vermouth are other options. Pimm's is a favourite summer drink. Tonic, American dry ginger ale, lemonade, cola and soda water are the usual mixers; Russian is a pomegranate-flavoured mixer that goes well with vodka. Have plenty of ice cubes and sliced lemons to hand.

After-dinner drinks may include a selection of liqueurs, Cognac, brandy and port.

Alcohol-free drinks

Have a plentiful supply of non-alcoholic drinks chilled. Still and sparkling mineral waters and jugs (pitchers) of tap water with ice and lemon are essential. Orange or tomato juice are

Below *Offer a selection of spirits for pre-dinner drinks.*

basic options, while apple, pineapple, exotic fruit and cranberry juices are popular. Alcohol-free beer is an acceptable alternative to beer.
• Add a generous dash of bitters to sparkling mineral water.
• Serve a squeeze of lime juice, lime slices and mint sprigs in tonic.

Beer

While beer is traditionally associated with informal barbecues and student parties, it is also an excellent drink to offer as an alternative to wine at drinks parties or as a pre-dinner drink on more formal occasions.

There is a vast choice of bottled beers available in most supermarkets. Coming from all over the world, they range from some light in colour and flavour to others that are dark, malty with a rich deep flavour. Fruit-flavoured beers are also popular. Colour and flavour are not necessarily related to strength – something to be especially aware of at parties – and some of the paler, light and fizzy beers are extremely strong.

Make the most of any specialist local breweries that offer particularly good or unusual beers not readily available outside the area. As well as selling live beer on its yeasty sediment, in casks or by the bottle, or bottled "bright" beer without the same level of active yeast (and therefore to be consumed within a couple of days), specialist breweries usually prepare seasonal beers. For example, for a limited period they may offer refreshing summer brews or warming winter ales. When buying a cask, always take advice from the brewery on the delivery and setting up of the barrel or storing the beer before the party, if appropriate.

When beer is offered as an alternative to wine, a light, lager-type brew that is thirst quenching and not too strong usually appeals to most tastes. This type of beer is good for barbecues, homely cooking (such as pasta dishes and meat sauces) and spicy meals (Mexican or Indian dishes, for example).

Fruit-flavoured beers are a good choice for drinks parties. The rich ales and very dark beers – such as British stout or the famous Irish Guinness – are a good alternative to red wine with robust, hard cheeses, such as mature (sharp) Cheddar. They are also excellent with meaty stews and casseroles and are popular instead of wine for informal lunches and suppers.

Light beers should be served well chilled. Darker beers are usually served cool – at cellar or cool room temperature – rather than chilled. However, this is a matter for personal preference and many prefer dark beers lightly chilled. Tall, slim lager glasses or large, stemmed balloon glasses are ideal for light beers. Larger tankards are traditional for the darker beers but they are not necessarily ideal for parties, when tall tumblers are much more practical.

Glasses

Disposable cups may be cheap and good for avoiding washing up but they do absolutely nothing for any drink, wine, spirits or otherwise. Even the most humble wine tastes better from a decent glass and a pleasing glass is one that is well balanced to hold, sturdy enough to feel safe but not chunky, and with a fine rim from which to sip. The bowl should be big and it should taper in towards the mouth to capture the aromas given off by the wine.

Conventionally, white wine glasses are smaller than red, which was thought to have more aroma and body to occupy a part-filled glass, but there is no good reason for this as whites are just as pleasing to swirl and sniff before sipping. The best solution for dinner parties is to have large white wine glasses and extra-large glasses for red.

Champagne and sparkling wines should be served in tall, slim, straight-sided flutes. These are designed to hold the bubbles, or mousse, of the wine for as long as possible, keeping it sparkling down to the last sip. The champagne saucers of the Sixties – wide and shallow glasses – allow all the bubbles to escape from the large surface area of the wine.

Fortified wines are served in smaller quantities, so smaller glasses are used, but they should still be large enough for the aroma and substance of the wine to be appreciated. Old-fashioned sherry glasses and even smaller liqueur glasses are sad receptacles.

Tumblers and tankards

In addition to wine glasses, medium to large plain tumblers (250ml/8fl oz/ 1 cup to 300ml/½ pint/1¼ cups) are basic, ideally the smaller ones for shorts and mixed drinks and the larger for water, soft drinks, juices, cider or beer. Large-bowled wine glasses with sturdy stems are excellent for light beers, cider

Above *Wine glasses are a preferable option to disposable cups.*

and substantial soft drinks. Tall, larger glasses are good for light beers, retaining the fizz and being well balanced to hold. Straight-sided glasses holding 600ml/1 pint/2½ cups are preferred for larger quantities of beer; jugs (pitchers) with handles or tankards are also satisfying for large amounts.

Quantities

A bottle of wine yields six average glasses. The amount consumed at a dinner party depends entirely on the company, ambience and attitude. It is always better to have more wine than needed and more than one bottle of each type than too little. When serving a selection of wines, remember that some guests may prefer to drink all white or all red rather than change with the courses. On average, allow one bottle for two non-drinkers.

When catering for a large gathering, calculate the number of glasses based on six from a bottle. When serving sparkling wine as an introductory drink, allow extra unless the wine will not be served until everyone is gathered, as those who arrive first will probably consume slightly more. When selecting

Above *Serve beer in tall tumblers, pint glasses or tankards.*

special wines, such as good champagne for a large special-occasion party, it can be worth buying from a supplier offering sale or return. At informal parties, both large and small, it is common for guests to bring a bottle.

Below *One bottle of wine will provide around six average glasses.*

Classic Cocktails

The cocktail party can be a fun occasion for a Twenties or Thirties theme or a sophisticated contemporary gathering. If you are planning a fancy dress party, write fun invitations and ask guests to dress in style. Go to town on decorative, colourful cocktails, with novelty cocktail sticks, swizzle sticks and straws. Follow the theme through with music from the era and encourage guests to dance. Conversely, adopt a stylishly understated approach to a contemporary cocktail party, with smart drinks, canapés and nibbles. Keep the music low and lighting discreet, and concentrate on circulating and instigating stimulating conversation.

The cocktail bar

Invite guests to join in the mixing and shaking at a fun party, with the bar working from the kitchen. For more sophisticated gatherings, arrange a trolley or small table from which to shake, stir and pour, then use the kitchen as back-up. Hiring a good bartender will be worth every penny as long as the cocktail list, numbers and shopping list are discussed and agreed in advance.

Below Cocktails will add colour and endless variety to a drinks party.

Whether the party is fun or formal, focus on a few cocktails based on a limited number of drinks, and stick to that list. Have a recipe sheet and all decorations or accessories ready. Include a number of alcohol-free drinks.

Cocktail equipment

Bar measures and a small measuring jug (pitcher) are useful. The traditional single measure is 25ml/¾fl oz/1½ tbsp and the double is 45ml/1½fl oz/3 tbsp. If you do not have specialist measures, use a small sherry glass or similar. A set of measuring spoons is also essential.
Shaker: you will need several cocktail shakers for a party. Look out for those that have integral strainers. Make sure the shakers have tight-fitting tops and that they pour well.

Above The choice of equipment is vast but you only need a few essentials.

Mixing jug (pitcher): use for drinks that are stirred not shaken – look for one with a good pouring spout.
Blender: a goblet blender is useful for frothy cocktails. Do not crush ice in the blender, as this will blunt the blade.
Strainer: for straining mixed drinks into glasses.
Muddler: a long stirring stick with a bulbous end, which is used for crushing sugar or mint leaves.
Mini-whisk: a long-handled balloon whisk with a small balloon for whisking and frothing drinks.
Citrus squeezer: look for one with a deep container underneath and a good strainer to keep out the pips (seeds).

Zester and cannelle knife: these are usually combined in the one implement. Use for paring fine shreds of rind from citrus fruit. The cannelle knife cuts individual, slightly larger but thin strips and can be used to mark a pattern in the fruit rind. When sliced the rind forms a decorative edge.

Nutmeg grater: a small, fine grater for grating whole nutmeg.

Straws, swizzle sticks and decorative cocktail sticks: just some of the finishing touches for decorating drinks.

Glasses

Cocktail or martini glass: the classic V-shaped cocktail glass keeps warm hands away from cool drinks. This holds about 100ml/3½fl oz/½ cup.

Collins glass: the tallest of tumblers with narrow, straight sides, this holds about 250ml/8fl oz/1 cup.

Old-fashioned glass: the classic whisky tumbler, this is wide and short and it is referred to as a 175ml/6oz/¾ cup tumbler.

Highball glass: this is a 250ml/8fl oz/1 cup tumbler.

Liqueur glass: the smallest of glasses, this holds about 50ml/2fl oz/¼ cup.

Below A wide variety of different shaped glasses are suitable for cocktails.

Above Small whole fruit, such as cherries or strawberries, can be used as decorations.

Brandy balloon or snifter: the rounded shape is designed to be cupped in the hands to warm the contents while the narrow rim traps the aroma of the drink.

Large cocktail goblets: these vary in size and shape. Designed for serving longer or frothy drinks, these glasses have wide rims.

Champagne glasses: either saucers or tall narrow flutes. The flute is the best for sparkling wine and champagne cocktails; the saucer can be used for a variety of cocktails or drinks.

Red wine balloon: holding 250ml/8fl oz/1 cup, this should be filled about half-full to allow room for swirling the wine and releasing its aroma.

White wine glass: a long-stemmed glass held by the stem, so that warm hands keep away from chilled wine.

Pousse-café: a thin and narrow glass with a short stem, this is used for layered and floating cocktails.

Below Slices of lemon or lime add colour and flavour to many cocktails such as a Moscow Mule.

Drinks Checklist

Familiarize yourself with the flavours before writing your cocktail menu. The following is a basic guide:

Brandy: Cognac and Armagnac are the two French brandies. Fruit brandies or eaux-de-vie include peach, cherry and apricot brandy.

Champagne: dry (brut) champagne features in many cocktails. Champagne has the best mousse for making excellent fizzy cocktails, but less expensive sparkling wines, such as Spanish Cava, can be used instead.

Gin: familiar as an aperitif with tonic, gin is used in a variety of cocktails. It is flavoured with juniper berries.

Rum: dark rum is punchy but light rum is clear; this type is used for cocktails.

Tequila: a powerful Mexican spirit distilled from the juice of the agave cactus. Used in a variety of cocktails.

Vermouth: dry white, sweet white or red, or bittersweet rosé, there are many brands of these herb-flavoured aperitifs. The more expensive brands are generally better quality.

Vodka: as well as the basic, slightly peppery strong spirit, there are many varieties of flavoured vodkas, some subtle with herbs or spices, others distinct with fruit. A good quality plain vodka is useful for most cocktails.

Whisky: basic whisky is good enough for cocktails rather than masking the flavour of a long-matured single malt.

Liqueur flavours

Amaretto di Sarone: a sweet almond-flavoured liqueur.

Anisette: aniseed-flavoured liqueurs include French Pernod, Italian sambuca and Spanish anis.

Bénédictine: made by Benedictine monks of Fécamp in Normandy, this golden liqueur is flavoured with myrrh, honey and herbs.

Chartreuse: originally made by Carthusian monks at La Grande Chartreuse monastery. This brandy-based liqueur is available as a green or yellow drink. Herbs, honey and spices flavour the liqueur. Yellow Chartreuse is flavoured with orange and myrtle.

Cointreau: orange liqueur.

Crème de cacao: cocoa-flavoured liqueur.

Crème de cassis: blackcurrant-flavoured liqueur – add a little to chilled dry white wine to make kir or use it to flavour champagne for kir royale.

Crème de menthe: mint liqueur.

Curaçao: orange-flavoured liqueur that is available coloured blue, clear or orange-brown.

Drambuie: malt whisky liqueur with herbs, honey and spices.

Galliano: golden liqueur flavoured with herbs, liquorice and aniseed.

Grand Marnier: French Curaçao, flavoured with bitter bergamot, orange and brandy.

Kahlúa: Mexican coffee-based liqueur with a rich flavour.

Southern Comfort: sweet fruity liqueur based on bourbon whisky.

Above *Strawberry and banana daiquiris are popular cocktails.*

Crushing ice

In the absence of an ice-crushing machine, lay out a clean dishtowel and cover half with ice cubes. Fold the other half of the cloth over, and then use a rolling pin or mallet to crush the ice fairly coarsely. Store in plastic bags in the freezer. If necessary, crush the ice finely just before using it.

Below *Crushed ice can be prepared in advance and frozen until ready to use.*

Making decorative ice cubes

These are particularly good for enlivening simple cocktails and mixed soft drinks.

1 Half-fill ice cube trays with water and freeze until firm.

2 Dip pieces of fruit, olives, citrus rind, edible flowers or mint leaves in cold water, then place in the ice cube trays.

3 Top up the trays with water and freeze until hard.

Below *Ice cubes with edible flowers.*

Frosting glasses

This simple technique adds a decorative and/or flavoured edge to the glass. Instead of sugar, the rim can be dipped into celery salt, grated coconut, grated chocolate, coloured sugar or cocoa powder. The flavouring depends on the type of drink you intend to serve. Place the frosted glass in the refrigerator until it is required.

1 Hold the glass upside down so that the juice does not run down the outside when you wet it. Rub the rim of the glass with the cut surface of a lemon, lime or orange.

2 Keep the glass upside down, then lightly dip it in a shallow dish of sugar, coconut, salt or celery salt. Re-dip the glass, if necessary, so that the rim is well coated.

3 Turn the glass the right way up and leave to stand for a while until the rim has dried. Chill in the refrigerator before pouring the drink into the middle of the glass.

Basic sugar syrup

Some cocktails include sugar syrup. This can be made in advance and stored in a sterilized airtight bottle in the refrigerator for up to 1 month.

1 Mix 175g/6oz/scant 1 cup sugar and 600ml/1 pint/2½ cups water in a heavy pan. Heat gently, stirring, until the sugar has dissolved.

2 Brush the inside of the pan with cold water to clean any splashes of sugar that may crystallize.

3 Stop stirring and boil for 3–5 minutes. Skim off any scum and, when it stops forming, remove from the heat. Pour the cooled syrup into sterilized bottles.

Traditional Cocktails

Knowledge of a good selection of classic cocktails is essential, and some favourites are given here, but you may also enjoy creating your own.

Black Velvet: combine equal parts Guinness and champagne.

Bloody Mary: mix 1 part vodka with 2 parts tomato juice. Stir in a dash of Worcestershire sauce or Tabasco and add a squeeze of lemon.

Brandy Alexander: shake together 1 part brandy, 1 part crème de cacao and 1 part double (heavy) cream. Serve dusted with freshly grated nutmeg.

Buck's Fizz: serve 1 part freshly squeezed orange juice topped up with 1 part champagne.

Daiquiri: shake 15ml/1 tbsp lime juice with 45ml/3 tbsp white rum and 5ml/

Below Bloody Mary served with celery, olives and cherry tomatoes.

1 tsp sugar on crushed ice. Pour into a sugar-frosted glass. Add fruit if desired, such as banana or strawberry.

Dry Martini: shake 2 parts gin with 1 part dry white vermouth. Pour into a glass and add a stuffed green olive. Some prefer to reverse the quantities, with 1 part gin to 2 parts vermouth.

Harvey Wallbanger: place some ice in a tall glass and add 2 parts vodka and 6 parts orange juice, then float 1 part Galliano on the surface.

Long Island Iced Tea: Mix equal parts vodka, gin, light rum, and tequila (optional) and lemon. Sweeten with a little sugar syrup and top up with cola. Serve on ice.

Manhattan: Mix 1 part each of dry and sweet vermouth with 4 parts bourbon or whisky.

Margarita: shake 1 part Curaçao, 4 parts tequila and 1 part lime juice. Serve in a salt-frosted glass.

Above *Brandy Alexander.*

Above *Martini with olives and chillies.*

Below *Strawberry Daiquiri.*

Above *Harvey Wallbanger with orange.*

Above *Long Island Iced Tea with mint.*

Below *Perfect Manhattan.*

Above *Margarita with lime.*

Below *Blushing Pina Colada.*

Pina Colada: shake 3 parts white rum with 4 parts pineapple juice, 2 parts coconut cream, 30ml/2 tbsp grenadine and 15ml/1 tbsp sugar syrup. Serve decorated with pineapple and a maraschino cherry.

Pink Gin: add a dash of Angostura bitters to a gin and tonic.

Rusty Nail: stir 2 parts whisky with 1 part Drambuie and serve on ice.

Tequila Sunrise: mix 1 part tequila with 2 parts orange juice. Pour 5ml/ 1 tsp grenadine into a glass and add ice, then carefully pour in the orange mix.

Whisky Sour: shake 1 measure whisky with the juice of ½ lemon and 5ml/ 1 tsp sugar on crushed ice. Pour into a tumbler.

Punches and Cups

Warming mulled wine, heady punches or delicate fruit cups are excellent welcome drinks for medium to large parties. Most well-seasoned party givers have their favourite recipes for a summer punch and a warming winter wine cup. The following are basic recipes to tempt you into experimenting further.

Mulled Wine: the classic Christmas drink for complementing melt-in-the-mouth mince pies. Stud 1 orange with 8 cloves and place it in a pan. Add 1 cinnamon stick and 60ml/4 tbsp sugar. Pour in a bottle of fruity red wine and add 150ml/¼ pint/⅔ cup brandy or rum. Cover and place over very gentle heat for 30 minutes. The wine should be just hot and aromatic. Taste and add more sugar if required. Serve hot.

Honey Glühwein: mix a handful each of raisins and blanched almonds with 1 lemon studded with 4 cloves, 1 cinnamon stick, 150ml/¼ pint/⅔ cup rum, 30ml/2 tbsp honey and 1 bottle red wine in a pan. Cover and heat very gently for about 30 minutes, or until the wine is just hot. Taste for sweetness and add more honey as required.

White Wine Cup: place 150ml/ ¼ pint/⅔ cup brandy in a bowl. Add ½ sliced orange, ¼ sliced cucumber and some mint sprigs. Cover and leave to macerate for several hours – this can

be left overnight. Add 1 well-chilled bottle dry white wine and top up with 900ml/1½ pints/3¾ cups chilled tonic water or lemonade.

Elderflower Strawberry Cup: rinse 4 elderflower heads and place in a bowl with 50g/2oz/½ cup halved strawberries. Add 750ml/1¼ pints/ 3 cups sparkling mineral water and 60ml/4 tbsp sugar. Stir well, crushing the elderflowers slightly and pressing

Below Cider punch with lemon rind.

Above *Serve refreshing white wine cup with ice and garnish with borage.*

the strawberries without crushing them. Cover and leave to stand overnight, then chill well. Strain the mineral water into a bowl. Add 175g/6oz/1½ cups sliced strawberries and a bottle of chilled sparkling white wine. Taste for sweetness and decorate the bowl with washed elderflowers before serving.

Cider Punch: place 1 sliced lemon, 1 sliced orange, 1 quartered, cored and sliced apple and several mint sprigs in a bowl. Pour in 300ml/½ pint/1¼ cups medium-dry sherry. Cover and leave to macerate for several hours or overnight. Add 1 litre/1¾ pints/4 cups well-chilled dry (hard) cider and top up with 1 litre/ 1¾ pints/4 cups sparkling mineral water.

Sangria: slice 2 oranges and 2 lemons and place in a jug (pitcher) with 150ml/ ¼ pint/⅔ cup brandy or Grand Marnier. Add 1 bottle red wine, cover and leave to macerate for several hours. Add 2 cored and sliced apples and top up

Below Warming mulled wine.

with 1 litre/1⅓ pints/4 cups lemonade and 600ml/1 pint/2½ cups orange juice, soda water, or sparkling mineral water (alternatively, use all lemonade).

Alcohol-free drinks

Although there is a wide choice of commercial soft drinks, there are many home-made cold drinks that are a real summer's treat for picnics or garden parties. Here is a selection:

Lemonade: grate the rind of 4 lemons and squeeze their juice. Place the rind and juice in a bowl and add 175g/6oz/scant 1 cup sugar. Add 600ml/1 pint/2½ cups boiling water, stir well and cover. Leave to stand overnight. Stir in a further 600ml/ 1 pint/2½ cups water, add 1 lemon cut into slices and some ice cubes. For picnics, carry the chilled lemonade in a bottle in a chiller bag.

Above *Sangria is a cool summer drink.*

Ice Cream Soda: place a scoop of good quality vanilla ice cream in a tall glass. Slowly add lemonade or soda water (lemonade is sweeter and tastes better

Above *Thirst-quenching St. Clements.*

even though soda water is correct), allowing the ice cream to froth up before filling the glass more than half-full. Decorate with berries, add a straw and long spoon and serve immediately.

Strawberry Banana Shake: purée 115g/4oz/1 cup hulled strawberries and 1 banana with 50g/2oz/¼ cup caster (superfine) sugar in a blender. Gradually add 600ml/1 pint/2½ cups chilled milk with the motor running. Pour into four glasses, add a large scoop of vanilla ice cream to each and decorate with fresh strawberries. For picnics, carry the chilled shake in a vacuum flask and omit the ice cream.

Mango and Lime Smoothie: peel, stone (pit) and dice 1 ripe mango, then purée it with the grated rind and juice of 1 lime. Add 600ml/1 pint/2½ cups chilled natural (plain) yogurt and whizz for a few seconds. Sweeten to taste with honey and serve immediately. For picnics, carry the chilled drink in a vacuum flask.

St. Clements: top up orange juice with an equal quantity of lemonade and serve with crushed ice.

Left *Old-fashioned lemonade is great at summer barbecues and picnics.*

Suppliers and Useful Addresses

Great Britain

Cake Art Ltd
Venture Way
Priors Wood
Taunton
somerset
TA2 8DE
01823 321 532
Wholesale suppliers of icings and equipment.

The Cooking Shop
The Old Estate Offices
Church Road
Sherbourne
Warwickshire
CV35 8AN
01926 624 444
www.thecookingshop.com
Kitchen supplies, accessories and equipment.

Epic Creative Limited
The Studio
38 Acacia Close
Stanmore
Middlesex
HA7 3JR
020 8954 3311
www.epic-creative.co.uk
Catering service.

The Garden Furniture Centre Ltd
Yew Tree Farm Craft Centre
Wootten Wawen
Henley-in-Arden
B95 6BY
01564 793 652
www.gardenfurniturecentre.co.uk
Suppliers of exclusive and innovative garden furniture and garden products.

Great Little Parties Limited
20 Burners Lane
Kiln Farm
Milton Keynes
MK11 3HB
01908 266 080
www.greatlittleparties.co.uk
Children's parties suppliers of invitations, party bags, tableware, balloons, gifts, candles and games.

Hobbycraft
0800 027 2387
www.hobbycraft.co.uk
Arts and crafts materials and equipment.

Invicta Bakeware Ltd
Westgate Business Park
Westgate Carr Road
Pickering
North Yorkshire
YO18 8LX
01751 473 483
Bakery equipment.

Non Stop Party Shop
214–216 Kensington High Street
London W8 7RG
020 7937 7200
www.nonstopparty.co.uk
Suppliers of party accessories, tableware, balloons and novelties and themed accessories.

Paperchase
213–215 Tottenham Court Road
London
W1T 7PS
020 7467 6200
www.paperchase.co.uk
Stationery, greeting cards, art materials and gift packaging.

Squires Kitchen
Squires House
3 Waverley Lane
Farnham
Surrey GU9 8BB
0845 2255 671
www.squires-shop.com
Specialist in sugarcraft and cake decorating products.

USA

A Cook's Wares
211 37th Street
Beaver Falls, PA 15010
800 915 9788
www.cookswares.com
*Bakeware, foods, appliances, pans,
cutlery and general utensils.*

Bowery Kitchen Supply
The Chelsea Market
460 West 16th Street
New York, NY10011
212 376 4982
www.bowerykitchens.com
Cooking supplies and equipment.

Broadway Panhandler
477 Broome Street
New York, NY 10013
212 966 3434
www.broadwaypanhandler.com
*Cooking utensils, knives, cookware,
bakeware, pots and pans and electrics.*

Chef's Catalogue
800 884 2433
www.chefscatalog.com
*Cookware, electrics, tools, bakeware
and cooking accessories.*

Party Suppliers & Rentals
4013 Oleander Drive
Wilmington
North Carolina 28403
910 791 0024
www.partysuppliers.net
*Supplies rental tents, tables, chairs,
party equipment, linens, china and
glassware and staging.*

Sur La Table
Catalog Division
1765 Sixth Avenue South
Seattle, WA 98134
800 243 0852
www.surlatable.com
*Bakeware, glassware, cook's tools,
housewares and specialty foods.*

Canada

Acme Tent Rentals
6999 Victoria Avenue
Montreal
514 342 5272
www.celebrationgroup.com
Quality rental equipment.

Gervais Rentals Inc
6570 Avenue l'Esplanade
Montreal. QC
H2V 4L5
514 273 3677
*Rental equipment for parties of any
occasion.*

New Zealand

Butler Gibpat
138 Ponsonby Road
Ponsonby, Auckland
PO Box 90998
AMSC Auckland
www.butlergibpat.co.nz
*Bakers supplies, catering equipment,
hotel and motel suppliers, kitchen
fittings and design, kitchenware and
restaurant supplies.*

Carlton Hire Group
0800 662 000
www.carltonhiregroup.com
*Cutlery, crockery, glasses, linen, tables
and chairs, marquees, sound and
lighting hire equipment.*

Australia

Barbehire
1236 Canterbury Road
Punchbowl
NSW 2196
02 9750 3390
www.barbehire.com.au
*Party hire for all occasions, catering
equipment, barbecues, marquee and
tables and chairs.*

Local Party Hire
38 Arden Street
Waverley NSW 2024
02 664 1399
Catering and party equipment rental.

Oxford Art Supplies
221-225 Oxford Street
Darlinghurst
NSW 2010
02 9360 4066
Arts and crafts suppliers.

South Africa

Jem Cutters
PO Box 115
Kloof
KwaZulu-Natal 3640
031 701 1431
Food supplies and manufacturer.

Index